Easy Mindfulness

Essential Strategies to Meditate, Reduce Stress, Heal Mental Health and Find Peace in Your Everyday Life

Dan Evans

Table of Contents

Prologue…………………………………………...............6

Chapter 1: What Your Body Tells You…..……... 12

Chapter 2: How to Start Meditation……………..37

Chapter 3: The Heart of Mindfulness………….....66

Chapter 4: Chakra Meditation ……………………95

Chapter 5: Somatic Mindfulness and Kundalini Meditation ………………..………………………...122

Chapter 6: Emotional Resilience and Self-Regulation…………………………………….…...142

Epilogue... …………………..………………….....192

Prologue

"Mens sana in corpore sano" is the famous Latin phrase for "a healthy mind in a healthy body" and the main concept of the Hippocrates philosophy. Hippocrates is the father of medicine, so he surely knows what he is talking about. Nowadays, most people do not have the time or the knowledge to listen to what their body is saying. The reality of the matter is that your mind listens to your body and your body listens to your mind. For example, if we feel bad about the way we look or we think we are facing problems with a dietary plan we are following right now are all thoughts and worries that start in our mind. Our body takes on these bad thoughts and the hidden beliefs that are behind those thoughts and you may suffer either from a reduced appetite or from an enhanced one.

There are many models and people who suffer from anorexia and when they look at their bodies in the mirror, they get sad or depressed because they think that their bodies are not beautiful or that they do not deserve this body perfection. Our bodies are composed of cells and each one of them "knows" whenever you are sad, happy, angry, displeased, etc.

Our bodies hold and protect our life if something goes wrong with it, then things may not end up well for us. Listening to them is not that hard and it is completely different than you needing your body to be healthy. For example, if you don't ask the help of an expert, you may think that by cutting off all the things that you deem unhealthy and eat only a specific type of food, you will keep your body healthy. This is not the case and this is the reason we must gather every piece of information available on how we can be healthy, if we can't visit an expert, and unnecessarily place our health in danger.

Many people follow strict diets wanting to lose weight. The problem with this way is that when you are so focused on counting calories and how many steps you walked this week, you will be unhappy because you will not listen to your body and your mind that may have given you signs of how wrong this situation was such as hunger pains and unhappiness. Why people gain weight when they are finished with strict diets? Because when the diet is over, they think they are free to do whatever they couldn't do during the time they spend imprisoned in a strict diet.

In this book, you will be guided through how you can successfully understand your body through many practices such as meditation, mindfulness and many more. You will explore the signs of certain serious conditions that could help you avoid letting the symptoms get worse and the problems of following a strict diet on your body and training methods that will keep you healthy.

In the first chapter, we will analyze what are strict diets and the effects they have on a physical and psychological level since they are the number one threat that prevents you from listening to your body because they promise a complete makeover. We will also analyze the signs your body sends you on various common conditions such as lactose intolerance to provide you with some useful hints on what it means to listen to your body. In the second chapter, we will examine how meditation will help you in listening to your body. In addition, we will analyze everything that is important to understand about meditation that will help beginners in their first steps at the practice as well as present you with numerous basic exercises, to begin with. In the third chapter, we will introduce you to the benefits of mindfulness and how it can help you with your task of listening to your body effectively.

In the fourth chapter, we will provide you with the necessary information about the seven chakras that exist in our bodies and how you could use them to achieve the desired result. In the fifth chapter, we will talk about Somatic Mindfulness and Meditation along with Kundalini Meditation and the tools they are able to provide to reach your goals. In the sixth chapter, we will present you with the necessary information on how to develop your emotional resilience and how to maintain it. You will also be provided with the necessary information to develop your self-regulation skills as well as everything you need to know to maintain them. Let us start our journey then!

Chapter 1: What Your Body Tells You

Dieting has been an integral part of people's quest on how to lose those extra pounds they have gained. Counting how many calories each food you eat has, keeping notes of everything that goes into your mouth, and choosing to follow a strict diet almost always has the exact opposite effect of losing and maintaining the lost weight on a long-term scale. Dieting and eating healthy are opposite.

Many people choose to follow diets, they do so because they actually work but in the short term. They are most appropriate for people who have reached completely unhealthy levels of weight, and those people need to lose a certain percentage of fat in order to avoid any possible fatal danger and when the dieting is over to start eating healthy and maintain a healthy lifestyle.

The good news is that according to studies, fewer and fewer people follow diets and start eating healthy instead, mainly because they have learned their lessons from mistakes of the past. People all over the world have started to understand that if your plan to lose weight does not seem possible to maintain for long, then you should not even bother starting in the first place.

However, how would you know if your diet is bad for you? By learning to listen to your body and the signs, it sends you whenever your diet is wrong and it needs to be changed immediately. Those signs vary from subtle to downright obvious, but they will always be there since the plan of your diet will influence your body on a much bigger scale than you could ever imagine. What we place inside our bodies will affect your skin, your mind, and how productive you are during the day. There are not a few cases of people whose diet and their body shows them that their diet is not appropriate for their health. Let us see all those signs that your body tells you to stop this dietary plan and start eating healthy.

One sign of bad dietary plans is bad breath caused by Ketosis, the result of metabolic process that happens when glucose, a source of energy, is not enough in our bodies and our metabolism burns fat. These results in creating acids named "ketones" that can make your breath smell bad. People who follow low carb diets are more prone to accumulate ketones to their breath and these diets and ketones can be extremely dangerous for people that have type 1 diabetes. They should visit a doctor because ketones may mean that there is not enough insulin in their bodies. The problem will be resolved if you increase your eating portions so that the required energy you need is taken through food. On the other hand, bad breath can be caused also from smoking, coffee, and by not caring for your teeth enough.

If your hair is thinning, it means that your iron levels are low. Iron is essential to the production of red blood cells and they in turn transfer oxygen throughout our blood. If your iron levels are low, you may feel sluggish and your hair will get thinner. Eating green vegetables such as broccoli and spinach, and red meat will enhance your iron levels. For women, iron levels could fall even further due to menstruation and not only due to bad diet programs, so they should follow a dietary plan that is full in iron.

If you notice that you suffer from continual diarrhea, you may have Coeliac disease. Coeliac disease is a reaction of our immune system from eating gluten found in barley, wheat, and rye. Our small intestine is triggered by eating gluten and can lead to weight loss, abdominal pain, and diarrhea. If you cut off gluten from your dietary plan, the problem will be resolved and keep in mind that Coeliac disease is completely different from gluten intolerance even though they have the same symptoms.

If you feel constipated, it is your body's way of telling you that you are not drinking enough water and your diet is lacking in fiber. For regular and normal bowel movement, both water and fiber are needed since the fiber is able to attract water, which in turn transfers it in the body in an easier way. In such cases, drink more water and at the same time add to your diet high fiber foods, like whole grains, nuts, beans, and dried fruit.

If you feel constantly tired and that your energy levels are low, there is a high chance that you are taking into your body too much sugar. Too much sugar or other carbohydrates can make you feel tired all the time and for you to have low energy levels. This happens because the sugar will raise the insulin that is in your body at first, but if you have a daily intake of more sugar than necessary; it will cause your energy levels to fall. Do not believe that when you feel less energetic it is right to eat more sugar. On the contrary, reduce your sugar and your energy will elevate and stabilize in no time.

If you are going to the toilet frequently to release fluid, you are dehydrated. Often people think the opposite is true, but even if when you drink too much water, your bladder is full and triggers the brain, signaling you that it is time to relieve yourself, this is not always the case. Your bladder may also be irritated by your urine is concentrated in one specific location. The solution to this problem is to drink much more water in order for your urine to be clearer than yellow.

If you constantly feel as if you are swollen all the time, this is a sure sign of your following a bad diet plan. If you feel gassy, especially after eating dairy products, you might even be lactose intolerant. There are signs that will tell you if you suffer from this condition such as nausea, vomiting, gas, diarrhea and cramps in the abdomen area that will begin from thirty minutes to two hours after eating anything that contains lactose. Lactose intolerance is happening because lactase, an enzyme that is produced in our small intestine, is insufficient in our bodies.

Even though many people exist, whose lactase levels are low and have no problems in digesting dairy products without any problems, there are also those who face the mentioned symptoms after they eat dairy foods. In this case, the lactose contained in the food you eat is directly transferred into the colon without first being processed and absorbed. When it reaches the colon, undigested lactose encountering normal bacteria, resulting in the signs of lactose intolerance.

When you are always hungry at the end of the day by following a specific diet, then you are not following the right diet for you and your body suffers along with you. After a day of successfully following your diet plan, nighttime is another matter. You may be so hungry that even your willpower is not strong enough to keep you from a bag of chips. Eating excessively is caused by your body's demand that it doesn't get all the necessary nutrients needed to be full and healthy. Keep in mind that a proper diet with the purpose of being healthy and right for people, should not eliminate food groups unless it is necessary for medical reasons.

A psychological sign of you following the wrong diet plan is if you are constantly in a bad mood. Food cravings will irritate you when you are trying to cut down your carbs and calories. In addition, the sugar in your blood is low during this process, a fact that contributes to severe mood swings.

Research has shown that diets consisting of low carb consumption can have a severe effect on your thyroid, which is responsible for the temperature of your body. If your thyroid slows down, you will feel cold even during summer. Try not to cut down all carbs. Just make certain that you include in your diet complex carbs such as whole grain bread, and more other foods like pasta.

Another sure sign of an unhealthy diet is wrinkles and acne. Diets that are lacking vitamin A will have a huge impact on your skin since vitamin A has an essential role in controlling the production of retinoid. Any deficiency caused to this nutrient could also drive you to have brittle nails and dry hair. To solve this problem, eat foods that are rich in vitamin A such as carrots or sweet potatoes.

Mental illnesses may stem from a bad and unbalanced diet. If you feel depressed all the time, you may follow a diet that is not providing you enough minerals, vitamins and Omega-3 acids. Your mood can be changed by taking nutritional supplements with vitamin B12. They are usually prescribed to patients that are trying to tackle mental illnesses.

Memory can also be affected by eating badly. According to researches, saturated fats had an effect on women who showed lower memory abilities and were slower on thinking tests when compared to those women that did not eat those saturated fats. If you want a sharp memory, you should do well to avoid fast food and French fries.

Our immune system is affected by a bad diet. For example, you may always be sick if you follow a low-protein diet since proteins help you by reinforcing your immune system. If you ban essential nutrients of your body, you will weaken your immune system and therefore you will leave yourself open to illnesses. Make sure to stay healthy and eat many proteins such as lean meats, and beans.

When you have a small cut or even a larger injury, you may have noticed that it takes more time to heal than the time it takes on other people. For a wound to heal fast and appropriately, it requires a considerable amount of nutrients to be in your body, so if you heal slowly it may be because your nutrients are not enough to help through the process. A bad diet can and will affect the resilience of the new tissue, the time you will need to recover from a wound, no matter how small it is, as well as how effectively your body will battle an infection that may affect the wound. Research has shown that proper amounts of protein, nutrients, and calories are needed for wounds to be healed effectively.

The above are signs of the physical kind your body is showing you to indicate that something is wrong with your diet and your overall health. However, our body includes our mind and hence the emotional responses to a bad lifestyle. We mentioned how depression can be enhanced by strict diets and generally following a bad lifestyle.

This can also happen when it comes to anxiety. Although your way of eating is not scientifically proven that can cause an anxiety disorder, it may make the symptoms of anxiety worse. Strict diets for weight loss may lead you to anxious moods as well as restricting calories along with proteins. In addition, overeating will cause the same effects because it will lead to weight gain. Eating too little or too much will increase your anxiety because you will never be satisfied with the ending result. A balanced diet will resolve this problem since you will see the desired results in your body as well as in your emotional responses.

Anxiety disorder can be revealed through physical symptoms that will warn you of the condition. There are many types of anxiety disorders such as panic disorders, separation anxiety, generalized anxiety disorder, phobias, social anxiety, and obsessive-compulsive disorder that have unique symptoms linked to fears that each type of anxiety can produce. Generally, anxiety disorders have many common physical symptoms and your body will express them to warn you of the danger.

These signs include nausea, stomach pains, digestive trouble, tiredness and fatigue, sleep issues such as insomnia, headaches, shortness of breath or rapid breathing, sweating, increased heart rate, muscle pain or tension, shaking or trembling. For example, if you are going through a panic attack you may feel dizzy, develop chest pain, have trouble breathing, and feel as if you are choking, or feel as though you may pass out.

Keep in mind that anxiety is how the body responds to stress and alerts you to potential threats that you should be prepared to deal with. For example, you may breathe faster because your lungs are trying to take in more oxygen just in case the need arises to escape from a situation.

Stress can be caused by bad eating habits. People who follow a strict diet are more prone to develop emotional stress than those who follow a balanced diet. Fewer calories and carbohydrates are likely to multiply stress since both are essential for the brain to work correctly as well as to produce a number of chemicals that make people feel good, like serotonin. However, eating more food than is necessary for our bodies can also enhance stress because we gain weight and therefore we may get depressed by our image and stress out to lose this extra weight by following strict and unbalanced diets.

What happens when we suffer from depression? What are the physical symptoms that warn us of this disorder? Most people are aware of the emotional symptoms, but our bodies react to depression too to warn us of the dangers we are placing ourselves into. Depression causes constant and persistent emotions of sadness and a lack of interest in things about your life that you previously loved. This is the main reason why depression is a dangerous mood disorder since it can lead you to think that life is not worth living anymore.

The physical symptoms of depression include back pain and headaches that if they existed before as migraines they will probably get worse. In addition, you will endure chest pain, but it may also occur due to a serious lung, heart, stomach condition. You may also have diarrhea or be constipated for long periods. Added to this, you will feel tired as if getting out of bed is an impossible task, no matter how much sleep you get.

However, people who suffer from depression, are not able to sleep as well as they did before. They may not even be able to fall asleep once they retire for the night or wake up too early while other people may sleep much more than they normally did, before developing depression. Finally yet importantly, depressed people will notice a change in their appetite, which will result in either losing weight or gain weight. The result is different for every person.

The above are some of the signs our bodies will show us when we follow a bad diet, when we have lactose intolerance, when we have anxiety or when we suffer from depression. What happens though, when our body has to warn us that our overall health? How will your body tell you that you need to make different lifestyle choices and take care of it more? There are signs that will show you when the time has come to take responsibility for your body and start listening to it.

Your skin will show you if you take care of your health appropriately. With the exception of people who are diagnosed with skin issues such as acne, bad skin will tell the tale of your overall state of health. If you keep seeing blemishes or stretch marks, it can be the result of a bad diet or lack of a daily skincare routine and cleanliness.

Sleep is extremely important for following a healthy lifestyle and if you are not able to sleep at night, there can be many reasons for this occurrence such as getting less caffeine, following a bad dietary plan, and not letting out much energy during the day that prevents you from falling asleep. Eight hours of sleep, a day is required for us to stay healthy and productive throughout our lives. Pinpoint the problems that are causing your body to refuse to get the rest it needs and make the necessary changes.

Low vitamin levels can be expressed through constantly chapped lips, bad fingernails and toenails or skin problems. If you have to apply lip balm in order for your lips to seem healthy, then you need a vitamin boost. Make the necessary changes to your diet and when you get the appropriate nutrients, you will notice your lips improving too. Usually, chapped lips indicate a deficiency of vitamin B-2 or else riboflavin. This vitamin is necessary for healthy nails, skin, and hair. You can get vitamin B-2 by eating dairy products, vegetables, eggs, nuts, beans, and lean meats. Adult males need 1.3 milligrams of vitamin B-2 while adult females need 1.0 milligrams of vitamin B-2 in their system.

Another vitamin your body needs and when not found in appropriate numbers in your system may cause chapped lips, skin problems or swollen tongue is vitamin B-3 or else niacin. To receive the needed amount of 13 to 20 milligrams of vitamin B-3 per day, you need to eat foods such as beef, poultry, tune, been, milk, vegetables, and halibut. An insufficient amount of vitamin B-6 or else pyridoxine can also be a sign of skin problems and cracks found at the corners of your mouth. Adult women and men up to 50 years of age should receive 1.3 milligrams of vitamin B-6 every day from food such as legumes, meats, green vegetables, and whole grains.

Another physical sign your body shows that you are not healthy is cold feet and hands. Even though the environment you live in may be the cause, if you constantly feel that your hands and feet are cold, it may be considered as a sign of cardiovascular problems, specifically circulation issues. In other words, there is not enough blood flowing in certain places in your body.

Another sign you should watch out for is if you have noticed that you are getting shorter. As we age, it is normal to lose our height, but when this is happening earlier than is considered normal and in extremely small amounts, it can be a sign of a serious health problem such as bone loss. Another condition that can be attributed to this situation is not receiving enough essential nutrients such as calcium and protein. In the long term, this condition may lead to loss of the density of the bones and fractures.

When your legs swell, it may be a way of your body saying that there may be a problem with your kidney, heart or thyroid condition. Thyroid problems are also indicated through your neck swelling and specifically, your thyroid may be overactive when your neck swelling happens unexpectedly and at an extreme speed.

For women, dark and coarse hairs that grow on the chin may be a sign of polycystic ovary syndrome. A hormonal anomaly can also affect a woman's period and thus a woman's fertility. Other signs of polycystic ovary syndrome are skin issues from enhanced levels of androgens, irregular period, and weight gain at the area around the stomach, trouble sleeping, depression and/or anxiety, and ovarian cysts.

In addition, if your big toe looks swollen and you haven't injured it in any way, it could be a sign and an early symptom of gout. Gout is extremely painful and can place you at the risk of developing chronic diseases such as kidney disease and elevated blood pressure. Another sign of gout is swollen joints, so if you notice these two symptoms happening for prolonged periods of time, a visit to your doctor is necessary.

When you wake up and you still feel exhausted, it may be a physical sign of restless leg syndrome, in other words, we wake up still feeling tired because our bodies never truly entered a relaxed state during the night. You may also have noticed an urge of moving your legs, especially when you sit down. A visit to your doctor will surely be a good move since he or she will point you in the right direction.

If you notice that you are sweating through your clothes and specifically on your underarms, face, or hands, you may have hyperhidrosis. It can be a sign of a medical condition, for example, an overactive thyroid, even though the sweat is harmless. If you also experience weight loss, fever, or shortness in your breath, you should visit your doctor because there are several medical reasons for your excess sweating such as lung or heart disease. You should start immediately by changing your diet and cut back on spicy food, curries, and garlic.

In addition, if you notice skin tags appearing in high numbers, it could be a sign of type 2 diabetes. They are caused by insulin-like growth factor 1 that is a protein commonly found in diabetes and can arouse skin overgrowth. If you also notice yellow bumps on your glutes, feet, joints, and hands it may be a warning of fat concentration under your skin. These spots are called xanthomas and are a warning that your blood fats such as cholesterol are extremely high. Another condition they can indicate is diabetes, some types of cancers, and pancreatitis.

Finally yet importantly, snoring is a common sign of sleep apnea that is linked with an increased risk of heart disease. Snoring is also linked to thickening carotid arteries in the neck and such damage can lead to heart attack and stroke. Studies have shown that snoring is found more commonly to people that smoke, have high cholesterol or are overweight.

If you push yourself and overdo it with your body, you might end up exhausted and do more harm to your body than good. If you don't listen to what your body has to say, how will you know what it needs and what should you do in order for you to live a healthy and long life? Do not be fooled by today's world. You may be busy and postpone your visit to the doctor since you think any symptom your body shows, will pass. You don't care about following a healthy and balanced diet because straining your body will get you the desired results faster, so how you look is the only thing that matters.

Keep in mind that your body will help you and be there for you if you take care of it. Your body is the house of your soul and it needs to be cared for as you take care of the house you live in. If your body thrives, you will thrive. If your body is healthy, you will be healthy. When we visit the doctor, we do so because we saw something. We noticed something was not going well within our body. So, how could you start forging this bond with your body? How can you start listening to it?

Chapter 2: How to Start Meditation

In the previous chapter, we mentioned the different conditions and problems your body is trying to warn you about, but many people do not know how to listen to the cues and others choose to ignore them because circumstances may suite this choice. However, it is imperative to master the necessary skills that will help you listen to your body and prevent further dangers to your health and general well-being.

The prevalent way of you being able to listen to everything your body needs to tell you is through meditation. However, what is meditation? Meditation an exercise for the mind that includes ways to focus, relax, and be aware of everything around you. Think of this as the equivalent of physical exercise but for the mind, not the body.

The definition of meditation according to psychology is "a family of mental training practices that are designed to familiarize the practitioner with specific types of mental processes".

Meditation is often done by a single person, in a seated position with the eyes closed even if it is practiced from a group of people, usually in cases of a meditation retreat. In addition, meditation is practiced through keeping your body completely still and your eyes closed even though there are practices such as Zazen and Trataka that let you keep your eyes open. This practice is extremely effective and helps you with your observation. In open monitoring meditation, you will be focusing on the environment around you in the present, allowing no disturbances or focusing only on one thing. In focused meditation that helps you with concentration, you will be focused on only one object. Meditation also helps you with your awareness levels that keep you focused on the present moment and you will pay attention to neither focusing nor observing anything.

Initially, meditation derived from the word "meditate" which means thinking strongly about something. All that changed as time passed until meditation came to mean what it does today, focusing your attention on thinking deeply. For instance, according to Christianity, meditation is a form of a reflective prayer that helps people create a bond with God or lets them think in peace, their religious beliefs. According to Buddhism, meditation is one out of the three methods that purify the mind and can lead to the achievement of Nirvana.

Therefore, in this case, with meditation, the goal for you is to achieve focusing and listening to your body. There are many meditation techniques to choose from and to find the one that corresponds better to your needs, you should try them all, practice each one for a week, and in the end conclude which one attains the best results for your goal. According to scientists, two categories of meditation are based on how you focus your attention.

In Focused Attention meditation, you will turn your attention on only one object for the duration of the practice. The object you will focus on is not necessarily a physical object. It can also be your breath, part of your body, images in your mind or a mantra. As you practice more and gain experience, you will be able to focus longer on the object of your choice and external distractions will be less frequent and shorter in time. In Open Monitoring meditation, your focus is not turned into only one object, but you will keep it spread on all parts of your experience, with no attachments. You will be able to acknowledge all your thoughts, memories, feelings and all sounds or scents from your environment.

Zen or Zazen meditation comes from Chinese Zen Buddhism and its origins can be traced to the 6th century CE. Zazen means, "seated meditation" in Japanese since you will find it practiced more commonly seated on the floor with your legs crossed. To all types of meditation, posture is extremely important. You can meditate when seated on the floor on a cushion or on a chair. Your spine should be straight all through your lower back, up towards your neck and you should not lean on anything. This is also the case for Zazen meditation. You will have to keep your mouth closed and your eyes barely open, resting your gaze at the ground that is close to you.

Zazen positions vary and the simplest one is Burmese Position, in which your legs are crossed and your feet are resting on the floor. The Half Lotus position is the one where your left foot is found onto the right thigh and the right leg is hidden under. In Full Lotus position, each foot is put on the opposite thigh. There is also the Seiza Position where you kneel on the floor with your buttocks resting on the heels of your feet.

During Zazen meditation, you can turn your whole attention to your breath, going inside you through the nose. Inhale and start counting from 10 backward for all the duration of the inhale and exhale process. When you reach number 1, start over again from 10 and in case you become distracted and get confused while counting, bring your attention back to ten and start over again. In Zazen meditation, breath is vital, the most important activity of the human body. Breath is one with the mind because when your mind is restless your breath is affected too by being agitated.

Another thing you can do during Zazen meditation is Shikantaza or else just sitting. In this form, you will not fix your focus on only one thing such as your breath, but you will try to stay in the present moment by being aware and noticing all the thoughts that pass through your mind while at the same time you do not ponder on anything.

Mantra meditation revolves around the mantra that is a word or a sentence without necessarily any particular meaning that the one who practices meditation repeats for focusing his or her mind. A mantra is not something used as a way for you to convince yourself that something needs to be done or is true. Teachers of meditation argue about the usage of mantra. Some say that the words used in a mantra as well as the correct spelling are extremely important because the sound of the phrase or word and the meaning have a vibration and the practitioner should be eased into a mantra. Some others say that a mantra is only the tool used for the said person to focus his or her mind and the choice of words is not relevant to the purpose of meditation.

You can also find Mantra meditation called "Om meditation" since that is the usual mantra used during the practice. Mantras can be found in Buddhist, Hindu, Tibetan, Taoism, Sikhism, and Jainism traditions. Other mantras that can be used when you practice is "om Namah Shivaya", "so-ham", "om mani Padme hum", "yam", "ham", and "Rama".

In this type of meditation, you are still in a sitting position with your back straight and your eyes are kept closed. You will repeat the mantra of your choice in your mind, without actually speaking the words, continuously until the end of the session. For as long as you keep repeating the mantra, it conjures a vibration in your mind that allows it to become more aware and delve into deeper levels of your awareness. In addition, as you keep repeating the mantra, there will be a time when the words will seem indistinct since you will be led into the field of consciousness.

The mantra will aid you to disconnect from your thoughts that keep entering your mind and you will reach a stage where no thought will interrupt your meditation time or the thoughts will be fleeting and as soon as they enter your head, they will leave. If you are not able to achieve this from the start, don't give up. It takes time for people to reach a level such as the above.

You may want to start for the first time by repeating your mantra aloud, to help you get used to it in a better and easier way. As soon as you are comfortable with your mantra, then start whispering it. It can be barely heard and the sound is barely there. Then, you can start saying the mantra inside your head. If you start using your tongue and throat at first, don't think of it as a wrong move. With practice, you will be able to stop moving those muscles and you will reach a level when the mantra will enter your mind without you trying to repeat it.

By repeating, the mantra at a fast pace, you will feel energized while when repeating it at a slower pace, your mind will feel and be calm. If you find random thoughts entering your mind that prevent you from reaching your goal, you may want to tune up the mantra. Speak it louder in your head or else your focus will not remain and instead you will be overwhelmed by troubled thoughts. Added to this, you can repeat the mantra whenever you inhale and exhale. You could also repeat it two times when inhaling and when exhaling. It all depends on how you feel and with what option you are more comfortable, for example, you could repeat the mantra by giving no thought to breathing.

According to research, people find it easier to maintain their focus while using a mantra than when they try to focus solely on their breathing. This is happening because when you repeat words into your mind, thoughts, sound, memories, and sensations are not that easy to interrupt you. You will be focused on your mantra, something that provides you with relaxation and awareness. You can also choose a mantra that means something to you. You want to start listening to your body, so you should use a word that makes you comfortable enough to attain this goal.

Walking meditation is another way for you could become more aware of your body. It is not as simple as taking a walk on the street since it is done at a much slower pace as usual walks and it requires focusing on our breath or other objects. In walking meditation, your eyes are open, your body is in a standing position and it moves, and you will be more in contact with the world outside. Since your body will be moving, you will be more aware of the sensations that flow through your body and you will be more grounded to the present.

When trying to choose a place for walking meditation, you need to keep in mind that you should practice it somewhere that is far from traffic and extremely populated areas. The place where you will be walking should not make you too distracted by the scenery so that your mind is able to be focused to meditate. At first, walking meditation may seem a bit strange, so it would be better if you practiced at your backyard or somewhere else that makes you feel comfortable.

The perfect length for walking meditation is at least fifteen minutes. It is easier to practice for more than a few minutes since you will not be seated or required to stay still. The slower you walk the better it will be for your focus. If you can't focus or you feel tense, try to walk even slower up until you are able to focus and ground yourself to the present moment. Before you start walking, it would be better if you try to connect with your body first by standing up and still while taking deep breaths.

Have your feet hip-width apart and let your weight fall evenly on both legs. The moment you feel stabilized on the ground, take a few deep breaths and let your eyes close. Then, focus on your body and try to feel everything, for example, how your body feels while you stand still and become aware of all the sensations that are flowing inside you. Even how the air feels on your hands is considered as being aware of your body. As far as walking meditation is concerned, we have several techniques to choose from.

The Theravada Walking Meditation is an integral part of Buddhist tradition when training. Many monks that reside in monasteries in Thailand walk for hours each day, developing their concentration. If you want to practice Theravada Walking Meditation, you have to pick a straight path with a distance of approximately thirty to forty feet. If you are able to walk it barefoot, it is highly recommended, but you can also wear light, comfortable shoes. Your back should be straight and your eyes lowered so as to when you walk, your attention should be focused on your feet.

Feel your legs muscles tense as you lift them and then lower them while walking and the sensations you feel through the air touching your whole body. Especially if you are barefoot, feel the sensations of each passing step as your feet come into contact with the ground. You should be aware of every part of your body since each step you take creates new sensations and leaves the old ones behind. When you reach the end of your path, stop, turn around, stop again and start heading back. Walk the path back and forth for as long as you wish and each time note your sensations. If you feel your mind wandering, focus back by asking yourself where you are focused on. During walking meditation, if you feel the need to stop for a moment, then do so, especially if intruding thoughts are too strong for you to not think about.

There is no right way of what you should fee. Each person experiences different sensations and emotions when practicing walking meditation. Your goal should be for you to connect with your body and the way it feels when you walk by focusing on each sensation.

Another type of walking meditation is Zen Walking Meditation or Kinhin. In Zen Walking Meditation you will have to walk a path of approximately forty feet long while maintaining a particular posture. It can also be done between breaks of seated meditation. You should stand with your back straight but not tense and your weight should be evenly distributed to each leg. Sense your feet touching the ground, take the Shashu position that is making a fist with your left hand, and grasp this fist with your other hand. Start walking the path while maintaining your focus on the movements of your legs and be aware of your mind instructing your body to move.

Your eyes should be lowered to not focus on anything and use your sensations to smell the air, hear the sounds of the path you are walking on and when you reach the end of the road, repeat the practice. Your pace should be relevant to the connection of your mind has with your body. For example, if you are tense, your mind may instruct your body to walk at a fast pace, don't try to change it. If your mind is at peace, it will instruct your body to move at a slower pace, don't try to change that either. It would be best to not think of the pace you are walking on while you practice Zen Walking Meditation, let your mind and your body to work that out alone.

There is also Mindfulness Walking Meditation, but this type of walking meditation will be analyzed in later chapters when we will talk about mindfulness as a way to listen to your body. Walking meditation offers a great opportunity for those who want to be more aware of the signs their body is sending them. It helps connect you to your body and mind and also offers you the necessary physical exercise for your body.

Meditation can be practiced whenever you want within the day. However, it is highly recommended to meditate early in the morning as soon as you wake up because the chances of skipping meditation practice later are high and because you will start your day with an open mind. It is also recommended, the place where you will practice meditation to be somewhere that makes you feel comfortable and where there will be as few interruptions as possible. When you practice meditation, your body should not be depleted of energy, so you should better not meditate after exercising your body or after staying for long hours at work. This also means that you shouldn't mediate when you feel the need to sleep and not when you have just eaten; you should wait about two or three hours after eating to mediate.

Before you start your practice session, you have to calm your body and relax it. Try to fill your mind with positive thoughts and emotions and if you find it difficult, remember your goal and try to do the previous two steps again. If during meditation, you get distracted, don't give up, it happens often when you have just started and it is important to feel happy when concentrated because you are letting all negativity go away and you are connecting with both your mind and body. When you are finished meditating, try not to end the session abruptly, instead, try to slowly move your arms, open your eyes, and move your legs.

In order for you to see results from this practice, meditation has to be repeated every day or else the benefits may be short and will not have the depth you'd wish to achieve. You need to search and discover if listening to your body is what you truly wish to achieve in order for you to commit to meditation. If that is your true goal, link it to meditation and think about how it will help you with getting better at listening to your body. Generally, meditation will help you focus, be more observant, and will teach you how to come in touch with all parts of your body.

To further enhance your motivation for practicing meditation, if listening to your body is not enough, there are many health benefits of practicing meditation daily. One of them is that meditation reduces stress and perhaps this is the most common and known reason people decide to start practicing it. When we are mentally and physically stressed this causes elevated production of cortisol, the stress hormone. In turn, this elevated production of cortisol causes the release of chemicals in our body, named cytokines. As a result, we can face problems sleeping, raise the chances of getting anxiety and depression, and contribute to fatigue.

Research has shown that meditation also helps to control anxiety. Since this practice helps us reduce stress, it also helps to better handle anxiety disorders, for example, social anxiety, phobias, and panic attacks. People, who work in professions that require a lot of pressure, choose meditation since it can also help reduce the anxiety that has to do with your work environment.

Your emotional health will too be improved since meditation can reduce cytokines that can affect your mood and/or lead to depression. To people who already suffer from depression, fewer cytokines will help them tackle this problem along with the help of their family, friends, and professional help. Meditation also helps you to identify the thoughts that are causing you harm since they may be filled with self-loathing and negativity. It makes you more aware of your thoughts, especially the negative ones, and enables you to leave them behind and turn them into positive ones by fixing the aspects of your life you hated before.

Your attention is increased and you are focused on something for a longer amount of time since you are required in meditation to focus on something whether it is your breathing or a mantra. Added to this, with continued practice of meditation, you develop a mental discipline that may help you fight various addictions you may have. You will enhance your willpower, learn how to control your impulses, and turn your attention to something that is more productive and healthy. You will learn more about yourself and why you intentionally harm yourself by indulging in these addictive behaviors.

If you had any problems sleeping, you will find out that by practicing meditation, your body will relax and therefore let all the tension of the day go, automatically bringing you in a peaceful and calm state which helps you fall asleep and not even wake up during the night by negative thoughts and unresolved problems. The health benefits are numerous and do not only concern listening to your body. Meditation also teaches you how to take care of your body which is essentially an integral part of reading the sign and listening to everything our bodies need to tell us.

Make no mistake believing everything is going to be easy at the beginning. You may feel the urge to give up because you believe that you are doing everything wrong or you don't have time for meditation. Like everything else, meditation needs dedication. Set a time, place during the day, and commit to it where you will focus only on practicing meditation. You could even reward yourself each time you complete a meditation session. Keep telling yourself that you are doing this to be healthier and form a bond with your body, something that you didn't have before.

Many people make the mistake of expecting to see immediate results too soon even though they may not practice meditation daily. It should be clear to everyone that decides to start practicing meditation that it should be practiced on a daily basis for you to witness the desired results. To make this point clearer, the length of your practice does not matter as much as consistency does. Five or ten minutes of practice every day is way better than an hour for two times each week. This is why most people who practice or teach meditation advise you to start in the morning before starting your daily routine. Even if your schedule is full, you could wake up earlier and practice meditation for three minutes at first if you can't make the session last more.

Many people have the same problem when practicing meditation that have with weight loss. They expect immediate results from the first day. However, you will never experience immediate results on both matters and if you expect to witness any benefits too soon, you will end up giving up in the end. Practice meditation without expecting anything in return, just go for the relaxation it brings and sees it as necessary as taking a shower every day. If you do it just because you expect to be less stressed by the first minute and don't learn how to enjoy it, then there is no point in starting practicing meditation in the first place.

Many meditation sessions fail because you don't prepare yourself before you start. Take a seat or before you start walking wait for a couple of minutes to calm your body and breath, and to connect with your mind. It is just like physical exercise, it is a mistake to start physically working on your body without stretching first. Also, keep in mind that there is a right meditation technique for you since different people are feeling better with different practices. For the first few months, you can evaluate different techniques, for example, you may prefer walking meditation instead of seated meditation, until you find which one is perfect for your personality and goals. If you keep trying different practices for a long amount of time, you may get disappointed because some may have different effects than the ones you actually need. Besides, it is better to find one practice and focus on perfecting it than struggling with learning them all.

Since you care to start meditation, don't make the mistake of thinking if you are doing it right or wrong. You will overanalyze your session during the time when you should be focusing on relaxing and connecting with your mind and body. If you find yourself wondering about this, you will interrupt your session by keeping your mind busy on different things than your actual session. In addition, this train of thought will sometimes drain you of the motivation needed to continue the meditation session because you will keep thinking how wrong you are doing it or how unsure you are if you are doing right or not. Just focus on the session and in time you will master the right way of meditating. The only thing two things you need to start is concentration and being aware of when your mind wanders off to irrelevant thoughts.

Another thing you should know for starting meditating is to start learning how to observe your state of mind. If you are plagued with problems that are not serious, such as breaking a cup, meditation will take more than normal to help you. In other words, for meditation to help you, you need to help yourself and not expect miracles to happen. We are taught how to meditate to keep our minds focused and calm, but if after you finish practicing, you let every little problematic detail into your mind to torture you, almost everything you have accomplished the previous minutes goes in vain. Think of meditation this way. You have been working out in the gym for an hour or two and the rest of the day you are eating junk food and having sugar-filled drinks. Would this help you have a healthier body? No. So, the same principle applies to meditation too.

Meditation will help with your job too. Your mind will be trained in being aware of your task at hand right at the moment that is given to you. You will learn through meditation what are your strengths, weaknesses, and talents. Your stress levels will be reduced and that leaves you with an opportunity to actually enjoy what you are doing without overthinking about certain things related to work. Not to mention that your productivity and work quality will improve since you will be able to schedule and prioritize your responsibilities better since meditation will enhance your self-control.

In addition, you could practice meditation with your family. Meditation will have a profound impact on your children's lives since it helps the brain function properly. It can also boost their energy and help kids learn how to keep their attention focused on any task they will be given. Meditation can also help them build kindness and love for themselves and for others. Children are able to learn anything at a faster pace than adults and have higher chances of maintaining the practice of meditation throughout their lives.

There are more types of meditation that will help you develop a deep connection with your body to be able to read the signs that are sent to you. However, they are too important and for this reason, will be analyzed in length in later chapters. For example, mindfulness is another essential part of learning how to listen to your body and is often confused as being the same thing as meditation. They may share some important values, but they also share important differences.

Chapter 3: The Heart of Mindfulness

Many people nowadays have heard of the word mindfulness and how important it is to be mindful. Many also have read that mindfulness and meditation is the same thing. Truth be told, mindfulness is not a new trend and has been present for thousands of years. It can be traced in Eastern religions like Buddhism and Hinduism and modern practitioners of mindfulness in the West have learned it from both the Buddhist and the Hindu tradition.

But what is mindfulness? The definition of mindfulness is the skill to be present and aware of the present moment. It is part of meditation that involves focusing your mind on being aware of where you are, what you see, and what you sense right now. There are four foundations of mindfulness that include Body Mindfulness, Sensation Mindfulness, Mind Mindfulness, and Mental Phenomena Mindfulness. As we said earlier, mindfulness and awareness are inherently linked together. But to be aware, you need to meditate since meditation is about awareness too.

The distinction between mindfulness and meditation may be tricky, but one difference is that mindfulness can be practiced everywhere, at any time, and along with anyone, the only thing you have to do in the most simple form of mindfulness is to be focused only on the present moment you enjoy with someone at any place. In addition, mindfulness can be practiced during meditation where meditation is only practiced at a certain time schedule and the person practicing it does so individually and in a relatively quiet and calm place.

Mindfulness offers you a better understanding, better health, and emotional recovery while meditation is able to offer all of these and add self-discovery, spiritual and personal growth. Overall, meditation is a big term that encompasses mindfulness since its goal is to achieve the maximum level of concentration and consciousness. Therefore, mindfulness is considered a part of meditation such as yoga, tantra, breathing, and silence.

The benefits of mindfulness will obviously include almost the same benefits meditation has to offer such as low levels of stress by the improvement of emotion regulation, it increases your focus, it helps you when dealing with sleep problems such as insomnia, it aides you in being productive to the workplace, it helps you control your anxiety, it will help you get over your addiction, it helps you relax, it nurtures your ability to feel compassion and it can also help you regulate your blood pressure. So, what do you need to know to practice mindfulness? To start with there are seven Attitudes of Mindfulness that you need to adopt, practice, and follow if you want to achieve true mindfulness.

The first attitude includes you to stop judging others. It is a fact that we live in a world where everything has to be black and white and passing judgments, however small, is taught to us since we were kids. To tackle this problem, start to notice whenever you are passing judgment both on yourself and on others. Try to lessen the times of this happening and you will see as a result that, surprisingly, you will start handling stress better. Passing judgment has its own form of stress; even subconsciously, we may feel obligated to judge what someone says or does. Added to this, when we pass judgment on a person, we may wonder if we were right or wrong and if we should feel guilty if we wronged that person. Stressful isn't it?

Another skill/attitude you need to develop is patience, which is extremely important for the rest of our life. Through mindfulness, you will realize that you have to let things unfold at their own pace and at their own time. There is no need to rush things or feel anxious whenever something didn't work out. When you are patient, you will no longer linger in the past or wait for the future to come as a child waits for Santa Clause. This happens because people think that their time should be full of activities for their lives to have meaning. Didn't you find yourself in a situation when you needed something so much you spent almost all your money on? Patience teaches us that this is wrong and we should be aware that the right to do something is or isn't that one.

The attitude of the beginner's mind involves our experiences now. It urges you to perceive everything as you are seeing them for the first time. This allows you to be open to new experiences and opportunities, to be happy for each passing moment you are and to be rest assured that you don't need to know every answer for every problem or question. Due to this mindset, you will become less attached to your past expectations that you have set for people or experiences and you will learn to be aware of many unique possibilities that come your way.

Trust in your feelings as well as in yourself, is the fourth attitude of mindfulness and an essential part of this practice. This part is where you are urged to search inside yourself, to find your insecurities along with your strengths and to tackle your supposed flaws as well as enhance your abilities. You will learn how to take responsibility for yourself and for your life by trusting yourself to make the right choices and if they are not, then you will learn to face your mistakes.

Non-striving is the fifth attitude that includes you not forcing certain things to happen and letting everything happen as they should. In other words, you should try less for something in order to attain more. That may sound outrageous since life is all about striving and going after what we want, but the goal here is to be yourself and not change your values to achieve something. For example, we are stuck in the past by wondering "What if" or "If only I had tried harder". The problem with these thoughts is that everything that had happened is in the past and we live in the present. There is no point to strive to change what already happened. We should embrace our choices as well as the mistakes we have done and live in the present.

Acceptance is the sixth attitude of mindfulness and it urges us to accept things for what they are without trying to change them. Trying to deny things that have happened or are about to happen will stress you out. Whether it is a breakup or death, we have to come to terms with what has happened. Acceptance allows us to take the necessary measures for the future and helps us stay focused on reality. It helps us see what we truly want and enables us to do it in the present.

Letting go is the final attitude of mindfulness and it teaches us that letting go of ideas, people, behaviors, or anything that keeps us from living the present moment is good for us. We cannot live our lives as they are in the present without letting go of the past or what holds us prisoners of enjoying every passing moment.

Mindfulness, like meditation, needs to be practiced daily, for as long as you are able to. There are many types of practices of mindfulness; some of them are Yin Yoga, Qigong, Mindful Eating, Body Scan Meditation, and Loving-Kindness Meditation. To start with, Yin Yoga is a type of yoga that includes slow paced sessions and the poses each person takes are maintained for longer than usual. This practice of mindfulness is stemming from the Taoist belief of yin and yang.

Yang depicts a change, movement, and revelations while Yin represents the unmoving, stable, and hidden part. This concept can also be practiced on our bodies. The stiff connective tissues of your body, the ligaments, tendons, and fascia, are seen as yin and the mobile muscles including our blood are yang.

Yin Yoga is about the Yin parts of our body, the connective tissues that respond better to slow exercises. For example, if you maintain a yin pose for a certain amount of time, longer than usual; your body will take the cue to make them a little stronger as well as longer each time. For beginners, the recommended time to hold a pose is up to three minutes each and with practice; you will be able to maintain a pose for five minutes. Some recommended poses are the Reclined Cobbler's Pose or Supta Baddhakonasana, the Happy Baby Pose or Ananda Balasana, the Supine Twist or Jathara Parivrttanasana, the Thread-the-

Needle Pose or Parsva Balasana, the Wide-Knee Child's Pose or Balasana, the Sphinx Pose or Salamba Bhujangasana, the Pigeon Pose or Raja Kapotasana, the Relaxation Pose or Savasana, and the Legs Up the Wall Pose or Viparita Karani.

When you change poses, you should be mindful and focused on your breath as well as the sensations your body has during each pose. If you find some poses to be difficult, don't give up on them, as we said before one of the attitudes of mindfulness is to be open to new experiences. As you move from one pose to the next, do it gently and be careful to never stretch to the point of inflicting any kind of pain to yourself. In each pose, you have to maintain stillness and surrender yourself to each position. Yin Yoga usually consists of passive poses that are held for a long time on the floor and help you exercise your pelvis, hips, inner thighs, and lower spine, areas that hold connective tissues.

Qigong is an extremely popular method of exercise in Chinese medicine and includes a combination of physical exercise and meditation. A method promotes your health, your mental focus, and alleviates your stress. In addition, it helps you maintain your Jing or what we call essence, the energy reserves of our bodies. With this method, you will have to harness your energy by allowing your twelve meridians to be open and accept the flowing energy. According to Chinese Medicine if one of your meridians is closed then there is a high chance of developing some kind of sickness in the area. The Twelve Meridians are:

- o Bright Yang Stomach Meridian of the Foot.
- o Greater Yin Spleen Meridian of the Foot.
- o Greater Yang Small Intestine Meridian of the Hand.
- o Lesser Yin Heart Meridian of the Hand.
- o Greater Yin Bladder Meridian of the Foot.
- o Lesser Yin Kidney Meridian of the Foot.

o Faint Yin Pericardium Meridian of the Hand.

o Lesser Yang Sanjiao Meridian of the Hand.

o Lesser Yang Gallbladder Meridian of the Foot.

o Faint Yin Lung Meridian of the Hand.

o Bright Yang Large Intestine Meridian of the Hand.

o Faint Yin Liver Meridian of the Foot.

Generally, scientists have admitted that Qigong helps in the relief of Arthritis, Cancer, Asthma, Chronic Fatigue, Headaches, Fibromyalgia, and many more. Qigong is separated into two parts, the internal Qigong and the external Qigong. The internal Qigong includes following a set of breathing exercises and meditation to achieve or maintain balance of yourself by using your energy to send it inside your body, resulting in enhancing its ability to heal and work properly. External Qigong is about using the energy you have harnessed in your body and apply it to someone else in order to heal him or her.

For beginners, it is recommended they start with MaBu or else the Horse Stance. Many types of Asian martial arts use this pose and to start, you need to be in a wide position. Then, you must drop your hips down to the height of your knees while your back is still straight. Your ankles and your shin should be at a 90-degree angle and your knees should also be at a 90 degree angle with your shin and legs. Your feet should be 45 degrees outwards and your shoulders should be pulled back with your spine straight. Your head should face forward and your hands can be brought straight in front of you or you could bend your elbows behind your shoulders. This position should be held from ten to thirty seconds if this is your first time practicing it.

Another position that is recommended for beginners is Gongbu or else the Bow Stance that is also used often in Chinese martial arts. To practice

Gongbu, you should place one foot forward and bend the knee of that leg slightly. The foot that is left behind should face 45 degrees outside and keep your back straight. Your one hand should face forward while the other should be bent to the elbow and place it to the side of your body. This pose should be held at first from ten to thirty seconds until you are able to do it for longer.

You could also practice Qigong sitting. Find a place to sit that makes you feel comfortable. Then, place your one palm up, to face the ceiling and have it close to your belly. The other palm should face downward and should be placed above your open palm. The two palms should have a considerable distance between each palm as if a ball was placed between them. When you feel ready, move around both your palms as if you were trying to sense this imaginary ball and feel the energy as your hands move. Your movements during all practice sessions of Qigong should be slow and gentle.

Mindful eating is a method that will help you control your eating habits and lessen binge eating. Through mindful eating, you will be able to reach a level of awareness of the subtle cues your body is sending you that has to do with eating such as hunger and cravings. You will acknowledge which food you really like or dislike and learn how to use all your senses when choosing which foods are healthier for your body. According to mindful eating, there is no wrong or right way to eat since everyone's eating methods and needs are special.

It is different from diets, especially popular ones since mindful eating is not focusing on restricting calories, but it gives us a choice to enhance the body's ability to control our eating habits. Eating because you will crave something, emotional eating, and binge eating will be able to control when you practice mindful eating since those are some of the reasons people usually gain weight and involve eating without control and mindlessly.

The first thing you can do when you are trying to practice mindful eating is to slow down the pace you eat. Since mindfulness promotes living in the moment, be aware of it and acknowledging the sensations and demands of your body, you should slow down and stop eating when your body signals you that it is full. For example, you could take short breaks between your bites and chew slowly. While you eat, your body and mind communicate so as to see if it is full. Your body sends its signals to your mind approximately twenty minutes after you start eating and this is often the reason why we end up overeating. However, if you eat at a slower pace, you will give your body and mind the time they need to communicate the necessary signals so as to stop or continue eating. You could chew each portion of food twenty-five times and you should always be seated when you eat. When we eat quickly, we don't let our body process the amount of food we eat and we don't give the chance it needs to signal that it is full.

It would also help if we didn't listen to our minds when it comes to food and focus on our body and whether or not it is indeed hungry. Is your stomach growling or you feel you are low on energy? Many times we eat because we are bored, lonely, sad, stressed or frustrated. Other times we eat during a movie or when we sit at our computers or in the car and not actually because we are hungry.

You should also develop a time schedule on when to eat. If you randomly eat meals at any time during the day, you may end up missing some and your hunger will make you eat way more than you should. This habit could affect your sleep and make our brain develop cues that are not entirely healthy for us. To achieve scheduling your meals, you could cook and store the meals for the next day beforehand. Also, when you eat along with friends or family it could be helpful since you will slow down to engage in conversation and actually enjoy your food.

Do not go shopping when you are hungry because you will end up buying unhealthy food that is quick to cook and eat. Added to this, you should think of where your food comes from and only see it as a product you buy from the market. Thinking about the process the food needed to pass in order for us to buy it and cook it, will make you more mindful of it and also bring you closer to nature. You will more thankful that you are able to eat such healthy foods and your body will thank you too. Take a moment to express your gratitude to everyone responsible for bringing this food to your plate and enjoy the opportunity you are given to enjoy it with your friends and family.

When you feel hungry, try to note how your hunger starts and when it ends. What foods make you full and which foods you need to eat more in order to satiate your hunger. Keep those things in mind for the next time you go shopping and which meals you should cook for the next day to eat. Eat only when you are genuinely hungry and try to savor the taste of your food because it may make you discover new flavors you will love to eat and be useful for your next trip to the market.

Also, try not to skip meals because your developing hunger will make it more difficult for you to be mindful when you are eating and it will lead you to eat anything when you are able to. Drinking water before you eat will help you eat the appropriate amount of food you need for your body and keep you from eating a larger portion of your meal than it is necessary. Most importantly be present when you eat and enjoy the moment. Don't think of anything else that can stress you and lead you to stress eating. Focus on the eating procedure and be thankful that you are able to eat this food that many people worked very hard for you to have on your plate.

Body scan meditation is a great way to connect you with your body and recognize the physical signs of stress and discomfort you may feel such as back or shoulder pain, headaches, and muscle tension and relieve them to an extent. Some people may have the signs and not even recognize they are stressed or troubled by a situation. This usually happens because they are not in an emotional state to accept the fact and also don't know how to read or ignore the signs their body sends them that it needs a break.

Body scan meditation will help you turn your focus on the parts of your body and the sensations associated with them while gradually shifting your attention from one part to the other, from your feet to your head. As you scan your body, you will be able to bring awareness to every single part of it and notice any subtle aches or tension associated with it. Your goal will be to acknowledge those cues and take the necessary measures to alleviate the problem after you are finished practicing body scan meditation. You should practice every day for as many times as you can, especially when you feel the need to do it.

To practice body scan meditation you should find a place to settle and sit that makes you comfortable to be able to relax your body as much as you can. You could also lay down since you will be scanning your whole body and many people practice body scan meditation before they fall asleep, but if you are not able to do so, sitting on the floor or on a chair will do just fine. Then, you should let your body get used to the position and the environment by taking a few deep and slow breaths and maintain this slow breathing pace for the rest of the session. Focus on breathing from your belly and try not to let your shoulders rise and fall with each breath you take.

Then, move your attention slowly to your feet and start noticing the sensations on them. Are you noticing any pain? Acknowledge it as well as any emotions that go with that pain. Focus on those sensations that cause you discomfort and imagine the tension separating from your body through each breath you take and then vanish into thin air. Stay there for a few seconds after you have acknowledged those sensations visualized them leaving your body and move on to the next part when you feel ready.

Continue the same pattern with every area of your body, as you will gradually move up until you reach your head. If you feel any discomfort, pain or pressure, take deep breaths and imagine those uncomfortable sensations leave your body. When you are finished, you will feel the tension leave your body and as you keep practicing you will also be more aware of your body and any possible subtle pain or tension that may accumulate in the future. You can practice body scan meditation any time you feel stressed even if it is for more than one time each day.

Another part of being mindful and practicing mindfulness it the loving-kindness meditation method that is part of self-care and will help you enhance your abilities to forgive others and accept yourself for what it is, that includes your body too. When you practice love-kindness meditation, you will focus your pure, loving, and fair energy to yourself and to other people. You will experience some warm feelings of compassion and realize why loving yourself and others is so important for everyone to do so.

During the session of loving-kindness meditation, you will have to pick certain targets, including yourself, to aim with your loving energy. Pick any quiet time during the day you may have, even on your breaks at work, and try to make yourself comfortable in a seated position. Then, close your eyes and try to relax your body by taking a few deep and slow breaths. Visualize yourself feeling the effects of emotional and physical wellness as well as inner calmness. Imagine the love you feel for yourself, acknowledge it, and let it grow.

Take the time to thank yourself for what you have accomplished so far, no matter how small, and accept the fact that you are alright the way you are now. As you visualize those things, keep in mind that as you breathe in, you take inside yourself love and breathe out the tension you may have. If you find your thoughts being interrupted, redirect your attention back to the feeling of calmness and immense love. Let those feelings engulf you and become lost in them. Then, you can have a choice to stay lost in those loving thoughts or redirect your focus to your loved ones and experience the love and gratefulness you feel towards them.

When you are finished with your meditation, open your eyes and relish in the lingering sensations of this wonderful experience. You can repeat this session any time you want during the day and anytime you feel stressed or the need to feel loved and appreciated.

If you don't want to choose a particular mindfulness meditation type, you also have the choice to practice the basic mindfulness meditation method that will help you develop mindfulness and be mindful about each moment of your life. You should start by finding a quiet place that makes you feel comfortable and sit on the floor or on a chair. You need to have your back and neck straight but be careful not to be stiff. You should also wear clothes that make you comfortable to avoid distractions.

Set aside all thoughts that are linked to your past and to the future to allow your mind to focus on the present moment. Focus and become aware of your breath and feel the sensation of the air moving in, out, and around your body. Pay attention to every thought that comes and passes, even those that include anxiety, fear, or worry. It is important not to ignore them. If your mind wanders off to other things, observe the direction they are headed to and without judging yourself for this outcome, bring your thoughts back to the present moment and sensations. When you are finished with your session, sit still for a minute or more if you feel the need to, and be aware of the place you are at before getting up.

Being mindful is an important skill to enjoy the present moments we come across since most people do not appreciate them or live them to the fullest until they become a pleasant or unpleasant memory. However, keep in mind that moments come and go, but your body will always be with you and this is why it is extremely important to be mindful about your body too. As you practice mindfulness of any type, you can add to the session ways of being mindful of your body too.

For example, as you sit on the floor or on a chair in an upright posture you could turn your focus on the sensation of your whole body. Sense the contact of the floor or chair on your body and how it feels, sense how the clothes feel on your skin and how the air impacts your body. You could also turn your focus on the parts of your body that feel tight or relaxed, cold or heated, and so on. You can focus entirely on pleasant or unpleasant sensations of your body to relish in them or fix them.

If you practice mindfulness of the body in different places, notice how your body reacts in each location and after certain changes. When you are finished with your session try to stay focused on how your body feels during different situations you will encounter during the rest of your day.

Following the different types of mindfulness meditation will impact your life and the way you see the world in a great and pleasant manner. When you start seeing the results of connecting to your body and to your mind or actually letting them work together as it happens in mindful eating, you will be the witness of a change to a healthier lifestyle. There are several more methods that are able to nurture your connection to your body and train you in how to listen to it such as Chakra meditation and Somatic meditation both of which we will analyze in later chapters.

Chapter 4: Chakra Meditation

The Vedas are the oldest written scripts in India, which originate from 1.500 to 500 B.C and are recorded from the oral tradition of the upper class Brahmins. Form there we learn of the chakra system that was then spelled as chakra. At first, the meaning of the word chakra was "wheel", referring to the chariot wheels of the ruler that were called Chakravartins of that time and it was also used as a metaphor for the sun. There were some mentions of the chakras as they exist today in the Yoga Upanishads of the 600 B.C and in Yoga Sutras of Patanjali of 200 B.C.

The chakra system rose along with Kundalini Yoga inside the Tantric Tradition. The word Tantra is translated as a tool (tra) for stretching (tan). But what is chakra? Chakras are concentrated energy in our bodies; they are spinning "wheels" of energy. Humans have major and minor chakras and when most people talk about chakras they mean the main seven physical ones that we will analyze shortly. Each of the chakras we have in our body connects us to the Universal Life Force Energy of the Universe. The system of Chakras is essential for the energy to flow from the Universe right into our bodies. Aside from the seven main Chakras, we have twenty-one minor chakras all over the body which are grouped under ten bilateral minor chakras that are found to the hand, elbow, foot, navel, ear, shoulder, and clavicles.

Chakra meditation is essential for people who want to learn how to listen to their bodies since if we do not provide the necessary support to them with the right food and vitamins then we will have less energy in the body. On the other hand, when we take care of our bodies through physical means and mental exercises we will have enough energy to be as productive as we wish. Chakra meditation helps you with energy flow and feeling more energized than ever. What are the locations of the chakras and what are their characteristics?

We will start with the first chakra that is named Root Chakra or Muladhara, which stems from the words Mula that means root and Dhara which means support. The role of this chakra is to ground you with the earth, in other words, to connect your energy with the earth. The Root Chakra is located at the base of your spine and more specifically near your tailbone and it ends bellow your belly button. It controls your basic survival needs and when energy flows through this Chakra you are able to feel secure as well as confident that you are able to satisfy your needs. It is the Root Chakra's role to provide you with all the tools you need to survive such as emotional security. The color representing the Root Chakra is red and when it is balanced you will be connected to the full experience of being human.

When the Root Chakra is overactive, you will be anxious and jittery because you will feel afraid. Fear is used and linked to the natural need we have to survive, to be alive. For example, you may have a successful job that makes you financially secure, but you will be constantly afraid of the possibility of losing this job and your financial security when the Root Chakra is overactive. It will give your mind subtle cues of the need to survive, even when you do not face any real threat. On a physical level, you may feel lower back pain, problems digesting food or hip pain.

In the case where your survival needs are generally being met, then the Root Chakra may become underactive. This could lead you to daydream or feel less connected to reality and more connected to what could have been different in your life, to your dreams. This may not seem as a bad situation, but being balanced is extremely important to keep your basic needs under control. For example, if you are in a constant state of daydreaming, you may neglect your present needs and end up with an overactive Root Chakra.

The law of Karma rules the Root Chakra which means that each action you take will result in an equal reaction. To make sure that your actions have positive reactions, you can put your body to good use and determine the possible endgame of your choices. In other words, you should listen to the cues your body sends you since the Root Chakra is all about fulfilling your basic needs. Your body will feel either comfortable or uncomfortable when you are about to make a choice and evaluates the threat level corresponding to those decisions.

To balance your Root Chakra, except from chakra meditation we will analyze shortly, you need to engage in physical exercise, you need to give the necessary nutrition to your body by eating red fruits, and connect to the earth by gardening, walking barefoot in nature or start swimming. You could also take baths with essential oils such as Rosewood, Sandalwood, Cedar, Ginger or Rosemary for relaxation.

The second chakra is named Sacral Chakra or else Svadhishana which means "the place of the self". The Sacral Chakra is about the identity of one's self and whatever he or she chooses to do with it. Out of all the chakras, this is the one who has to do with creativity and all the forms a person can express it since it is responsible for bringing you creative energy. It is related to your emotions, so it is the one who enables you to enjoy every moment you live as well as your successes in every aspect of your life. The color associated with the Sacral Chakra is orange and is located below your belly button and reaches its center.

When your second chakra is balanced, you will be able to enjoy everything life will throw your way from relationships, good food to sexuality and creative activities without overdoing it. However, if balance is not achieved and your second chakra is overactive you will face problems such as addictions or excess eating that will lead you to feel guilty for enjoying things that were ought to make you feel good because those things will not be healthy anymore. They may lead to obesity or restlessness and guilty emotions that will prevent you from being yourself and express your creativity and emotions in a healthy way.

On the other hand, if your Sacral Chakra is underactive by your focusing on every detail of everything and not enjoy or be thankful for each moment you are able to live or not give yourself enough credit for everything you have accomplished, you may get depressed and feel as if you are not enough for anyone or as if everything you do will never be enough to succeed. You will lack inspiration and creativity, symptoms that will be harmful to your body and spirit. You can balance your second chakra by wondering if your choices are good for you and healthy.

Think about the consequences of your actions and let your body and mind guide you in the right direction. Emotions are an integral part of our choices, but sometimes we have to listen to our mind and body to choose the appropriate path for us. Enjoy life, eat healthily, and maintain healthy relationships. This way you will be able to energize your Sacral Chakra.

The third chakra is named Solar Plexus or else Manipura in Sanskrit which means "lustrous gem". The Solar Plexus is responsible for your identity, power, self-confidence, expression of your will, and mental abilities. There must be times when you found yourself in situations that you knew instinctively how right or wrong they were for you by some cues your body was sending you. Most people would call it gut feeling, but this is the power of your Solar Plexus when it reacts. It makes you feel physically confident about a situation you are in. The color associated with the third chakra is yellow and is located at the center of your belly button and reaches the upper part of your belly. When the third chakra is balanced, you will get a feeling of continues wisdom where you will know almost all the time what is right or wrong for you. You will be decisive and empowered to act as you deem appropriate without ever doubting yourself.

On the other hand, when the Solar Plexus is not balanced and overactive when the power you have over your life transfers into the lives of other people, you may get angry quickly before even thinking about the reasons that got you angry in the first place. You will feel the need to control every little detail of your life and the life of others, lacking a key element in your every day encounters and that is empathy and also, the ability to feel compassion towards others.

You will become manipulative and misuse the power you may have over others. When the third chakra is underactive, you will lose all the power you exercised over yourself and probably be depended on others, you may also feel insecure, you wouldn't have the power anymore to make decisions and confidence will give way to neediness. You will lack having a purpose in life and a sense of direction. You can fix all that by focusing on the things that you are good at. By focusing on your abilities and skills, you will build up your confidence again in order to feel empowered once more.

The Solar Plexus chakra is all about expressing yourself, your abilities both physical and intellectual, personal power, and your motivation to turn your dreams into reality. If you find that you lack in those aspects, make a list of everything that represents you and everything you excelled before this situation brought you down. Remember everything you had accomplished and make them happen once again.

The fourth chakra is your Heart or else Anahata Chakra which means in Sanskrit "unhurt". Since it is located on your chest area which includes your heart, Anahata Chakra is responsible for your feelings of love, compassion, and bringing color and beauty to your life. It is often referred to as the bridge that brings together your physical body with your spirituality because it is located exactly in the middle of the seven chakras and connects the lower chakras which are referred to as the physical world and the higher chakras which are the spiritual world. The Heart Chakra is also associated with the love yourself and the love you are capable to feel for other people as well as the world around you including animals and nature. Your kindness also stems from the fourth chakra too and can control the intensity of these emotions. The color associated with the Heart Chakra is green and when it is balanced you will be able to feel love equally for both yourself and the others, even when you will go through tough times.

At the times when the heart chakra is overactive, you will lose the boundaries you have set for yourself and start making choices that are not healthy for you all because of love. For example, you will place the needs of others ahead of yours and you will end up losing your self-worth and your needs will be unmet for long periods of time, something that will definitely be not healthy for you. Keep in mind that it is essential to treat yourself with the same amounts of love and kindness you give to others.

On the other hand, when your fourth chakra is underactive you will become distant from other people since you will feel as if it is really hard to get close and form a connection with anyone. This happens due to the fact that life tends to throw in our way a lot of heartbreak and at some point, you will have to deal with betrayal. Those moments should be faced as a teaching moment and keep the lessons of those situations close as to not repeat the same mistakes we did to the past.

However, it can be hard for most people not to take the results and pain of heartbreak personally for longer than necessary. You may even feel the need to build a wall around your emotions and forbid yourself from letting anyone get close to your heart because you will feel afraid of the past repeating itself. You may also feel as if you can't connect with your body and find it difficult to communicate your emotional needs with your physical needs.

To bring balance to your Heart Chakra, you need to start by bringing love back into your life. You could even take back some of the love you give to others when your fourth chakra is overactive or bring down the walls you have built around your heart and let people get close to you again. Most of all treat yourself right by appreciating you and remember everything you have been through as a lesson you had to be taught. When you are able to love yourself again, then you will succeed in letting people love you and return that love in a healthy way so as to not neglect your own needs. The key is in how you see yourself. If you love your appearance and personality, others will love them too.

What you need to keep in mind that your Heart Chakra is all about love for yourself and others, relationships, acceptance and compassion, change and forgiveness, and your ability to grieve and move on. Once you have mastered all those things through meditation and mindfulness, your mind and body will be open for you to read as easy as you breathe.

The fifth chakra is the Throat Chakra or else the Vishuddha which means "pure". As the name of the fifth chakra suggests it is located at the center of the neck and that includes the throat. It works as a passage through which flows the energy between the lower chakras and the head. The Throat Chakra enables people to express themselves and communicate effectively. It gives voice to a person's truth and thoughts. The energy to speak comes from the fifth chakra on a spiritual level since we all know how we are able to speak on a physical level.

The color associated with the fifth chakra is blue and when it is balanced you will be able to speak out what you believe clearly along with love and kindness. You will know the exact words you will need to speak for each situation you will find yourself in. Those around you will be inspired by your ability to know exactly what to say and by your kind and wise words.

However, your Throat Chakra may be overactive when you have tried for a long time to make your voice heard to the people that are close to you. You may have felt ignored for long or that others dismiss your opinions too often and you have tried to tackle this problem by speaking more intensely and louder. If that is the case and your fifth chakra is overactive, you will notice that you interrupt other people often when they speak and people may tell you that you love to listen to yourself speak since you will talk more than it is necessary to make your point. On a physical level, you may have symptoms of throat pain or persistent infections.

On the other hand, when your fifth chakra is underactive, you will never speak the truth you believe in and refuse to speak up. People may think you a quiet person by nature or shy and often you will find yourself unable to describe your emotions or find it difficult to find the courage needed to talk back to someone. An underactive fifth chakra occurs for the same reasons as an overactive chakra. You have been ignored and dismissed for too long. You can balance your Throat Chakra by thinking before you speak, especially about serious matters. For example, think if your words you are going to utter are true or necessary. Are they kind or they are intended to hurt someone? Practice describing your emotions out loud even if no one is around to hear you. It doesn't matter if people are not around, sometimes when we voice our emotions it is easier for us to accept them and acknowledge their existence.

An imbalanced Throat Chakra will result in you not being able to control the things you say and you will not be able to listen and understand what other people are talking about. You will be afraid of speaking to everyone including yourself, and even if you speak, your voice will be heard as small and insignificant. You may also end up telling lies to avoid analyzing a matter you have to discuss with someone and you will not be able to keep secrets or hold your word.

The fifth chakra helps you to express yourself, to be able to speak out and to communicate with others and with yourself. As important it is to listen to your body, it is equally important to listen to your emotions and let them connect with your physical presence in the world. Being in tune with your emotions as well as your body will make your life much easier and open up many more paths for you to solve any problem that may come your way.

The sixth chakra is called The Third Eye Chakra or Ajna which means "perceiving". It is located on the forehead and between the eyebrows; therefore it is used for intuition and foresight. The color associated with The Third Eye Chakra is indigo and is often associated with the pineal gland located in the brain and regulates the time you sleep as well as the time you wake up. The Third Eye Chakra is responsible for your vision, intuition, receiving information beyond the five senses that is often perceived as a psychic ability, it connects you to wisdom and insight, and it motivates creativity and inspiration in you.

When The Third Eye Chakra is balanced, you will be in tune with both the material and the spiritual world and it is very difficult for the sixth chakra to be overactive. However, when an occasion such as an overactive sixth chakra occurs, you will find yourself focused on psychic activities such as astrology, tarot cards, and paranormal occurrences. These activities will overwhelm you and keep you from experiencing and enjoying your everyday life. When your sixth chakra is underactive, which is more common, you will feel disconnected from activities that enhance your spiritual presence such as meditation that is needed to balance your Third Eye Chakra.

Generally, imbalance of your sixth chakra includes feelings of being stuck in the daily routine and not being able to see beyond your problems creating a dead end for moving on, not being able to make your dreams come true, and it will make your reject anything spiritual or beyond what we have used to believe in. You will be dismissive that there is more in life than having a routine to stick to and feel safe in. You will not be able to connect to nature or to your emotions as well as your body.

The seventh and final chakra is named The Crown Chakra or else Sahaswara which means "a thousand petals". It is located at the top of our head and is enables us to access higher levels of consciousness as we realize that there is more in life than personal prejudices. A person's consciousness is located in the seventh chakra, but it is more connected to the energy of the universe than with ours. The color of the seventh chakra is often white or deep purple. The Crown Chakra connects your energy with the rest of the universe and the task of balancing it is the goal of the Buddhist concept of reaching nirvana. The moment you achieve the balance of The Crown Chakra you have beaten pain and death.

A balanced Crown Chakra offers you pure consciousness, wisdom or acknowledgment of everything that is sacred. It connects you with the limitless energy and possibilities provided by the universe and liberate you from any limitations of the physical world. Last but not least, it offers you pure bliss and spiritual ecstasy. An imbalanced Crown Chakra can be seen as being completely out of tune with your spirit and express continues cynicism and condensation to everything that is sacred or even be completely disconnected from your body. This may result in finding solace and meaning to fantasies and dreams inside your head that will make you distant from reality and the present moment.

Meditation will help you open all your chakras and especially the first six since The Crown Chakra is not that easy to balance or energize. However, if you manage to balance all the other six chakras, you will not have to endure the consequences of an imbalanced seventh chakra. Except for meditation, you could also try using chakra stones which when you interact with will affect both your physical and mental health. The stones for each chakra are the following.

1. The Root Chakra: Smokey Quartz, Hematite, and Black Onyx.
2. The Sacral Chakra: Sunstone and Tigers' Eye.
3. The Solar Plexus Chakra: Pyrite and Jasper.
4. The Heart Chakra: Aventurine and Rose Quartz.

5. The Throat Chakra: Sodalite and Aquamarine.

6. The Third Eye Chakra: Lolite, Amethyst, and Fluorite.

7. The Crown Chakra: Moonstone, Clear Quartz, and Amethyst.

Now that we have analyzed the basics concerning the seven chakras that exist in our bodies, it is time to present how meditation will help you open up your chakras and as a result make you feel more energized and in tune with your emotions and body. The first step to chakra meditation is to find a quiet place and sit on the floor or on a chair still for a few moments while taking deep breaths. This way, you will leave the stress and tension behind you. This is the moment when you get in tune with your body and how it feels at the present.

When you feel in tune with your body and the sensations it gives off, bring your focus on the base of your spine and imagine a spinning, bright red light. Feel it move at the same time as you breathe and stand there for a moment with your focus drawn on it. Then, move your attention slowly up your spine and let it rest on the area below your belly button. There, you will witness a bright, warm, spinning orange light that is in tune with your breath too. You should also stay at this are for a few moments until you feel comfortable with it.

When you finish, move your attention slowly up to the area above your belly button. As you focus all your attention on this area, you will feel strong emotions radiating from it such as love, fear or calmness. You will witness a bright, warm and spinning yellow light and again, you should pause for a moment until you get comfortable in its presence. Then, move your attention up to your chest area and more specifically, to where your heart is. There, you will encounter a bright green spinning light. As you focus and connect with it, you may feel the need to place your hand above the spot where your heart is. Don't hesitate to do so, it will help you connect with the area more.

The moment you are finished, move again your attention up and to your throat. There, you will imagine the existence of a bright blue light that spins. In this area, you might feel the need to clear your throat or swallow. Don't try to stop yourself from doing that since it will be a natural response to turning your whole attention there, especially if you practice chakra meditation for the first time.

Then, move your focus to the space between your eyebrows where your third eye rests. You will encounter a bright, deep indigo light. The light also spins and will become brighter with each passing second. When you are done getting used to and connect with your third eye chakra move to the final chakra that rests at the top of your head. There, you will see a spinning violet or white light that is very bright. This is the light that connects you to the universe and therefore as you focus on it, you will feel at peace and a sense of calmness that may blow you away.

When you are done connection and being comfortable with the final chakra, take a deep breath and when you feel ready to open your eyes. Don't rise instantly, but take a moment to acknowledge your surroundings and get used to returning to the present moment.

Learning about the seven chakras and their meaning to our lives will help you get more in tune with your emotions, mind, and body. Everything in the universe consists of energy and we are not the exception. The process and success of listening to our bodies do not only include getting physical exercise and eating healthy but also includes our efforts to listen to every subtle cue it may send us through meditation and mindfulness.

Chapter 5: Somatic Mindfulness and Kundalini Meditation

By now, you may think that listening to your body is an extremely difficult process or even that you have no need to practice everything that was mentioned before because you already know everything there is to know about your body's cues to you. That may be true, but there are always things gone unnoticed by man people when it comes to their bodies. For example, there is one of the most basic responses our body possesses that we do not know how it works exactly and all of us have experienced. The flight-or-fight response.

The flight-or-fight response or else the acute stress response is a psychological reaction that happens when we are in the presence of something that is terrifying to us either mentally or physically. When this response happens, hormones are released throughout our body to prepare us to deal with the threat or run towards a safe place. The name of this phenomenon derives from our ancestors during the ancient times who would either stay and face any threat that came their way or flee. No matter the choice we make, our body prepares us to face the incoming danger.

When we endure extreme levels of stress, our nervous system is put into action because there is a sudden release of hormones. The adrenal glands are stimulated by the sympathetic nervous system and the distribution of catecholamines is triggered, which include both noradrenaline and adrenaline. The results of this occurrence are increased heart rate, breathing rate, and blood pressure. When the danger has passed, it will take between twenty and sixty minutes for our bodies to return back to normal.

Another sign of flight-or-fight response it flushed or pale skin. As the stress starts to get a grip on you, the blood flow to the surface of the body is reduced to start flowing to the brain, legs, arms, and muscles. This will result in you getting pale or to your face being flushed as blood will rush to your brain and head. Your pupils will dilate since the body will also prepare you to be more observant and aware of your surroundings during the time you will have to face a threat. So, dilated pupils will offer you a better vision. Last but not least, you may also sense yourself trembling since your muscles will become more tense and ready to take action.

The above was only one example of how our body works even in dangerous situations that we may not even know what kind of response we are having or why we are acting a certain way. Being in tune with our bodies and knowing how to connect with them is a necessary skill to develop and the process of doing so will help you find out more things about yourself that haven't paid any attention to. So, it is not always true that we know everything there is to learn about our bodies. To this journey, an important method we could use is Somatic Mindfulness.

Somatic Mindfulness will help us build a connection between our mind and body, especially in the areas that there was no connection. It enables us to use the responses of our body as a source of information about our current state and our emotions. It comes as no surprise that Somatic Mindfulness is used as a way to cure emotional traumas since it can be utilized as a way to enhance our ability to regulate the nervous system by helping us release the emotions we may have help inside us unconsciously and feel them in a physical level.

Somatic Meditation is met in Tibetan and East Asian Buddhism as well as in spiritual Taoism. As the name suggests, in Somatic Meditation the main tool used is the body and in a lesser amount, the mind. The concept behind Somatic Mindfulness is that your spirit, mind, body, and emotions are all connected together. When you practice Somatic Meditation, you will feel less stressed, less pain, less anger or frustration, and it will help you get over past traumatic events. Essentially you will be free of all the things that are preventing you from listening to your body and live a healthy life.

However, you should be aware that when you practice Somatic Meditation overwhelming and painful emotions of a past trauma will come back to you in order for you to deal with them. Don't be surprised or try to end the session because a past emotional heartbreak or shock will have to be dealt with eventually and through Somatic Meditation, you will be able to deal with this occurrence in a controlled way.

When you start your sessions of Somatic Mindfulness, try exercising for at least once a week for a two month period, even though it is recommended for you to practice more than once a week. But if you wish to practice other forms of meditation at the same time, you can opt for a once a week session of Somatic Meditation. After you have finished practicing each time, give yourself a minute or two before you start any type of interaction with other people. You need time to fully acknowledge and take in the experience you just finished doing because sensing your body this way for the first time will be a powerful experience. For example, you will need to ask yourself how you feel after the session is over, has anything changed in the way you hold yourself? Do you feel any different? When you answer these questions, you can open your eyes and focus on the room you are in for a few moments to focus on your new feelings and take in your surroundings, on how you see the world now. Is it different?

Before you start practicing, stand up and ponder on how you feel at the moment before you begin your exercises. Focus on how your breathing is and pinpoint the location of where you have focused your attention and energy. For example, how does your energy feel when you focus on it? Do you feel calm and serene or do you sense negative emotions and by extent energy that makes you unsettled and fidgety? What do you need to heal? If you don't feel anything there is no need to worry or give up thinking that you are fine. Those emotions may reveal themselves to you later and if they don't, then continue because Somatic Mindfulness will help you connect on a deeper level your mind with your body, spirit, and emotions.

The exercises start with grounding. Stand up and let your eyes not focus on anything. Watch the room without actually seeing it. Then, raise yourself slowly on your toes and drop down to your heels. Keep up this exercise in a slow rhythm while at the same time thinking that all your weight drops through your heels. Keep this exercise up for a minute or until you feel the jolts of your hips and lower back loosen considerably.

After you have finished with the first part of this practice, take a short break but do not break the position you are in now. Then, create a small bouncing in your legs by using your knees and letting them bend slightly. Turn into a straight position by pushing backwards again and softly shake your legs. Focus and imagine that his soft shaking rocks your whole body and moves through your hips, up to your shoulders and reaches your neck. Let this exercise relax your jaw, your tail bone, and lower back until the duration of one minute passes.

Once your jaw, tail bone, and lower back are relaxed, take a short break and bring yourself back to a standing position. Let your hands rest at the front of your thighs while you start focusing on your breath. Inhale slowly and as you do that bring your chin forward and softly move your hips backward. Then, move your upper body forward so that you have created an arch with your back. Stay in this position for a moment, for around eight breaths, and later, as you continue breathing slowly, let your head fall relaxed down. Then, move your tail bone under and forward, around your back until you bring yourself into the position you were when you started. During this exercise, your focus should be on your breaths and your spine, on how it moves.

When the above exercise is over, resume your standing position and slowly sway back and forth as a bamboo does when hit by a soft gust of wind. You will feel all the accumulated tension leave your body. If you happen to feel little tremors on your body, don't try to stop them. This is the way your body releases tension.

In the end, stay still for a moment and focus on the sensations you have inside and are finally able to notice now. Can you feel more relaxed and less tense? Do you feel any different your feet and legs? More charged with energy perhaps? More alive?

Let us take a look at another type of exercise. Start by standing and letting your eyes look but focus on nothing. Place one leg forward by putting down your heel first and later your whole foot on the ground. Then, shift your weight forward and on that front foot without letting your back foot leave the ground. As you step forward, reach out with the same arm as your forward foot, with fingers outstretched. When your foot is on the floor, close your hand as though you grabbed something and don't forget to breathe all the while. When you reached this position, one foot forward and a hand turned into a fist, pause for a while and then, bring yourself into a standing position by setting your foot next to the other, by releasing your grip and letting your hand loose on your side. Do this exercise for two minutes on one side and two minutes on the other side. During this practice, keep your focus on your hand, foot, and breaths.

When you have finished with all sides, don't move and stay in a standing position. You may start feeling the sway from the exercise starting on its own. Don't try to stop it, but go with the flow all the while checking on how you feel. Does your body feel any different?

One last type of exercise, we are going to mention here is the following. Start by bringing yourself in a standing position and focus on your breath. Then, take a deep inhale and as you let this breath go, make a shhh sound with your mouth. Imagine you are telling to someone to keep quiet. You can even make the sound if you want to. As you do it, focus on how it makes you feel, especially on the area that covers your chest and your stomach. This sound should last until your breath is finished and then take another deep inhale and repeat the process. Keep in mind that this should be done for approximately eight breaths. The shhh sound is extremely useful for the opening of the diaphragm which sometimes is tight on occasions such as being afraid.

Next, inhale again deeply, and now utter the sound mmm, as you let your breath out. Press your lips together and find the appropriate pressure that will create the most vibration for your whole head. Keep making the sound for as long as you can keep up and then repeat the inhale process for around eight breaths. You should shift your focus on the vibrations caused by the sound that can be felt in your head. The humming sound can stimulate the vagus nerve which is the main branch of the parasympathetic nervous system. This way we will be able to relax by resetting the over-aroused nervous system.

When you are finished with this exercise, stand still and straight for a minute and check the sensations of your body as well as your emotions that may be new and noticed now. Do you feel any shudders or swaying movement? Do you feel the need to stretch? Don't try to stop it or avoid it, do what your body wants and move along with it. Do you feel any different than before you started this exercise? Maybe you noticed a difference in your breathing or any change in your sense of space? Maybe now you are able to put words on those sensations you experienced.

As we were able to see, Somatic Meditation is centered on the body and seeks to develop the connection of your body and mind as well as your connection to them. So, pay attention to your physical responses during the session of you practicing Somatic Meditation and with practice, you will be able to see more results. Awakening your body will have a profound effect on how you view yourself and will make you appreciate your body more than you already do.

One last method we will analyze that will help you start listening to your body more effectively is Kundalini which is a Sanskrit term which means primal energy and is coming from ancient India to teach us about a form of energy that has been roped at the base of our spine from the moment we were born and is also the source of our life force. Kundalini may be freed from the base of our spine by spiritual practices. Kundalini meditation helps you channel your energy and release all the stress that exists in your body.

Kundalini meditation is a part of Kundalini yoga and its goal is to move energy throughout your body starting from your root chakra located at the spine. This energy that is placed there has to be set free and go through all the seven chakras that exist in our bodies and then leave through the crown chakra that is placed above our heads. When we release energy from our body through this process, we create a communication path for the mind and the body to tackle physical, spiritual, and mental problems.

To practice Kundalini Meditation, the first thing you need to do is finding a location that makes you feel at peace and where no one is going to interrupt you. Keep in mind that the best time to practice is in the morning as soon as you wake up because the chances of being bothered are less. Another appropriate time for you to practice is at night, right before you go to sleep so as to destress and recuperate after a tiring day. Bring a bottle of water with you and choose clean, comfortable, and fresh clothes that will not bother you during your practice. Before you start, set a timeframe of how long would you like to practice, it could vary from a few minutes to a few hours. However, for beginners, it would be recommended a length of eleven minutes.

Take a seat on the floor with your legs crossed or even sit on a chair but place your weight on your feet. If you want to be even more comfortable when you are on the floor, you can choose to sit on a pillow or a cotton blanket. In both positions, your back should be straight. Then, lower your eyes slowly until they are approximately 90% closed. Regulate your breaths and chant a mantra to focus. A good choice for beginners is the mantra "Sat Nam" which means "truth is my identity" and it helps you direct your energy. Say "Sat" as you inhale and "Nam" as you exhale and as you do this, focus on the words you say out loud or imagine them being written in your head. This mantra can be also used during stressful situations you have on any day. You will have your own mantra that signals your breaking away from an old state and reflect on the state you want to be at the exact moment you chant it.

Kundalini meditation will help you let the everyday stress you may get from a hectic work environment or from problems you may currently face, go and turn it into peace. It will also teach you the right way to breathe and open up the capacity of your lungs. Added to this, you will be able to concentrate in an easier way than you did before and any random thoughts you may have will be prevented so as to not disturb your balance. You will learn how to be aware of your body and connect it with your mind and your spirit.

It is believed that Kundalini meditation can also help people who suffer from various addictions, depression, phobias, fatigue, grief, anxiety, obsession, sleep disorders such as insomnia, learning disorders, compulsions, and stress. It is important for you to not give up on practicing even though it may seem hard at first. All you need is more time and practice to be able to reach a level where you will be satisfied.

We live in a world where we come face to face with constant change, even we change many times during our life and we may not even notice it. Practicing meditation in all its types and forms will let you tackle those changes in the best way possible, not to mention you will be able to identify the changing needs of your body. Imagine what it would feel like to notice any subtle change your body goes through, to know the signals of almost every need of your body. It would save us a lot of time and pain from searching what is happening inside us.

However, to take care of your body, you need to know how to develop an emotional resilience and constantly work on it. An essential part of self-care is developing the necessary skills to be prepared

and face any stressful situation whether it is
something serious or something light.

Chapter 6: Emotional Resilience And Self-Regulation

Emotional resilience is the ability to handle stressful situations. The more resilient is someone, the more he is able to adapt to change without having any lasting difficulties. However, people who are less resilient don't handle as well as they should the stress and many changes they could come across their lives whether they are minor or major. Experts say that people who can handle minor stress reason in an easier way, they can also deal with major stress crises in an effective way. So, we can conclude from the start that resilience has many benefits for our everyday survival and state of mind.

Before we start analyzing the matter of resilience and how we could develop emotional resilience, we should understand what exactly we are talking about when we say stress since this is a word we have mentioned numerous times throughout the course of this book. Stress is what happens when we face a threat or a major challenge in our lives and that triggers a specific biological response during which hormones and chemicals are released throughout our body. Stress is the very thing that triggers our fight-or-flight response because the body needs to either fight the very thing that stresses us out or run away from it.

If we see it from the above perspective, stress is not necessarily a bad thing; it helps us when we are threatened. Stress is the very thing that helped our ancestors survive and it can help us today to avoid dangerous situations such as meeting our project's deadline, make us react quickly when we come face to face with having an accident or help you keep calm whenever others are throwing a tantrum. The stressors, things that trigger the stress response vary from people to people and may not even share the same attributes. For example, many people like speaking in public, but others hate it and each one has his or her own reason for doing so.

Stress isn't always bad, but the cases of it having severe consequences is when people are exposed to it for a prolonged period of time and can both physically and mentally hurt those people who are exposed for so long to it. If you consider the fact that when people are exposed to frequent adrenaline surges can lead them to damaged blood vessels, higher risks of heart attack and stroke, anxiety, headaches, insomnia, weight gain, and high blood pressure, then stress is not a healthy condition to have for the rest of your life. Three types of stress are acute stress, episodic acute stress, and chronic stress among other types.

Acute stress is what usually happens to everyone. The body reacts immediately to a situation that is a challenge or a threat to someone. For example, this is what people experience when they escape from a car accident. It may also be the frightening and yet exciting feeling of riding a roller coaster or when you bungee jump. These occurrences of acute stress don't hurt your health under normal circumstances. It is believed that these situations may even help you since they practice your brain in developing the appropriate response to possible future stressful situations. However, there is also severe acute stress that will be extremely harmful to your health and this is what you get when faced with a situation that will threaten your life and can lead you to develop post-traumatic stress disorder.

Episodic acute stress happens when you encounter persistent episodes of acute stress. This is the case when you are anxious about things that are about to happen or that you suspect they may happen.

You may be unsatisfied with your life and think of it as chaotic with you jumping from one problem to the next and that is causing you recurring acute stress episodes. People, who work in professions such as police officers or firefighters that have to deal with high-stress situations, have such episodes. As it happens with severe acute stress, episodic acute stress can also take a toll on your mental and physical health.

Chronic stress is what happens when you are exposed to high levels of stress for a long period of time. It suffices to say that being stressed for such a long period of time, your health will suffer. More specifically you endanger yourself to developing depression, anxiety, cardiovascular disease, weakened immune system, or high blood pressure. You will also have to endure headaches, difficulty when trying to sleep, and an upset stomach.

It is a fact that stress can make it extremely difficult for a person to control his or her emotions even when they are facing mild cases of stress. Their personal relationships may suffer from expressing their frustration as well as their work is possible to suffer too. Stress is also linked to diseases such as lung disease and fatal accidents. Children that are suffering from chronic stress are more prone to developing mental illnesses if this condition is not treated appropriately.

Stress can also lead to premature aging and it weakens your immune system. High stress levels place a toll on the immune system, which in results makes you more exposed to catching a cold and have infections. The causes of stress are too many and vary from person to person. Some common examples can be living through a chronic illness, being the victim of a crime, having gone through an abusive relationship or an unhappy marriage, living in poverty or being homeless, and working in a dangerous profession.

When you are stressed, you may experience symptoms such as insomnia and other sleep related problems, chronic pain, losing your appetite or eating too much, having concentration problems or making decisions, fatigue, and feeling irritable or overwhelmed. You can start a stress management program to help you get through those difficult situations and not develop the serious problems we mentioned above.

Seeing what stress can do to people, it is imperative to learn how to develop the ability to be resilient when we face stress related situations and changes that can generate this response. The Latin word "resilio" is where the word resilience stems from and it means to retaliate. So, resilience is the way we hold ourselves to tackle the problems we face and move on from them as a stronger person. There are three parts of emotional resilience on which we can start building on this important skill. There is the physical element, which translates into good health, energy, and physical strength. There is the psychological element that has to do with self-confidence, self-expression,- self-esteem, and good thinking abilities and last we have the social relationships you have and how healthy they are, for example, are they based on communication and cooperation?

Emotional resilience is not a new concept to adults since this is something we are born with. For example, some people are not at all affected by changes that are not programmed and others cannot stand them. Also, emotional resilience can be affected by your age, gender, and whether or not you have experienced a past traumatic experience. The great thing about emotional resilience is that it is not a skill you can or cannot have. There are many levels to master and even if you manage to not develop emotional resilience to its fullest, still you will have done an amazing job and your life easier.

In many resilience training programs those levels that need to be conquered are taught with the endgame being for someone to achieve emotional awareness. To start with, one of the main characteristics and first step in your journey to be emotionally resilient is self-awareness. Self-awareness is the ability to acknowledge and be in tune with your own feelings, as well as possible inside conflicts that you have developed. Through your journey to achieve self-awareness, you will be able to understand better to what extent your feelings are responsible for your actions rather than throwing the blame to other or environmental factors. You will learn how to look for all the necessary answers inside yourself and take responsibility for your actions.

By practicing self-awareness, you will notice that your relationships will be better since you will finally be clear and certain about your needs and what you want. Your moods will also get better since it is extremely depended on your emotions and how you choose to think about yourself. As you become more self-aware, you will learn how to listen to your body, thoughts, emotion, and behavior as well as the relationship that exists between those four factors. You will communicate more effectively since you will get a better understanding of what you believe in and your decision making skills will develop more because many bad choices we make are the result of thinking when we were emotionally charged.

To develop self-awareness are a few steps that you need to follow and watch out for. One thing you could do is to notice the things that bother you on other people. This will help you actually pinpoint some of the habits that are bothering you about yourself since it is often pointed out by experts that some of the things that irritate us in other people are nothing more but a reflection of something we don't like about our appearance or personality. For example, that may be placing the needs of others ahead of our own or avoiding conflict even though we are right about something.

Another way that will help you developing self-awareness is the mindfulness meditation techniques we analyzed in previous chapters to learn more about your emotions as well as your body. Also, you need to watch out for not paying too much attention to details or think too much out of a situation that is not that important or affects you immediately. Added to this, you need to also identify the triggers that cause you unwanted emotions such as prolonged sadness, anxiety or shame about yourself.

For example, you may feel anxious or angry during social gatherings because you are afraid of other people judging you about your views, looks, and even on how much you drink. You may find out that before you identified the trigger that is causing you such emotions, you were going to extreme lengths to avoid this trigger and distract yourself. The point of self-awareness and at the end of emotional resilience is to identify the problems you have with yourself and fixing them so as to be able to endure the stress and changes that will occur throughout your life.

Also, you could ask your friends and family to give you some feedback on yourself. Nobody is perfect and sometimes we are not able to pinpoint the parts of our personality that needs extra work. However, the people that love may notice those parts as you are noticing theirs. Ask someone that loves you about those blind spots you are not able to see and try to work to make them better. Maybe you are not a very patient person or you are not expressing your needs and your emotions to the point of letting other people impose their beliefs on you. Fixing those blind spots will make you become more self-aware and emotionally resilient throughout your life.

By knowing your weaknesses as well as your strengths, you will be able to work on those things that keep you from reaching your goals and make you less self-aware and emotionally resilient. Set boundaries that will help you maintain your goal and not make you lose the progress you have made in being more self-aware. Understanding what your limits are is an integral part of self-awareness and at the end of conquering emotional resilience.

Persistence combined with the motivation to achieve your goals whether they are making your dreams come true or obtaining emotional resilience. Persistence helps a person develop the consistency needed to deal with external stressors as well as handling internal emotional conflicts, thus making him or her emotionally resilient. Self-control will also help you when you are trying to gain emotional resilience. People who have emotional self-control are able to harness their feelings and redirect them to a more productive activity, so they will be less affected by stress and will not let it affect their lives as much as other people let it affect them.

Emotional self-control is the skill many people have developed to manage the emotions that disturb them and remain productive, even when they are under stress and have to deal with situations that would cause other people to fret. To develop your emotional self-control, you should first let a small amount of time pass between your emotions and response to them. It may not always be easy to manage your emotions; however, you can control your response to them. Pause for a moment and let yourself think before you act on what you feel. If there is no need for you to respond immediately, then let yourself think and calm for twenty-four hours. Also, you should wait before passing emotional judgment until you are certain you have all the facts. Making assumptions about something when the information we have is limited may lead us to say the wrong thing or making a big mistake we may not be able to fix later on.

Optimism will also help you on your journey of developing your emotional resilience since when we see the positive aspect even in the most stressful situations; we are able to cope with them in a more effective manner. It is often noted that people who have strong emotional resilience are able to laugh at the difficulties they may face because it can prevent you from facing those difficulties as a threat and therefore change the way your body will respond to stress. Being optimistic and having a great sense of humor about life's tough times can be a life altering move in both a physical as well as an emotional level. But what are the characteristics of people with strong emotional resilience skills?

People who have developed their emotional resilience are aware of every situation they find themselves in, their emotional reactions, and how people around are behaving. They know that in order to handle their emotions, they have to know what is causing them as well as the reason why they are caused. They are aware, resilient, and able to maintain control even in difficult situations by finding new ways to deal with current or future problems. They understand that life is full of changes and challenges and that people cannot avoid every problem. What they can do is to be open-minded and able to adapt to changes.

They know how to practice a considerable amount of control over their own lives by not blaming others for their problems and mistakes. They know that every problem or mistake they make is theirs to deal with and do not depend much on others to offer them a solution, and even if they ask for a second opinion, they will act as they deem fit because they know that any action they take will affect the result of an event and it will also affect them. Even if our problems are caused by external factors, it is important to know that we have the power necessary to choose what to do next and that these choices will affect our current state, our coping abilities as well as the future.

People who have developed emotional resilience have problem-solving skills that are essential for handling crises since with those skills, resilient people are able to find the solution that has the least dangerous outcome. When most people are going through a stressful and dangerous situation, they fail to notice important details and take advantage of potential opportunities that may be provided in order not only to solve the problem but avoid future similar situations too. Problem-solving skills are an essential part of developing emotional resilience and the ability everyone should develop even kids and teenagers. For adult problem-solving skills will help them make better decisions and learn how to be more aware of a difficult situation without having to resort to stress and fear, waiting for the situation to pass.

So what should you do to enhance and develop your problem-solving skills? To start with you should focus on the solution and on the problem you face at the moment. It is pretty simple as a step and the explanation behind it is just as simple. You cannot let your brain think of solutions when you turn your whole attention on the problem. When you focus on the problem instead of the solution, you are feeding yourself with negativity which in turn is translated to negative emotions.

Those negative emotions are responsible for you not being able to find potential solutions. Acknowledge the problem and try to remain calm. Then try to focus on the possible way you can deal with the problem instead of overanalyzing while wondering whose fault was that or what went wrong. As soon as you have dealt with the problem effectively, you will be able to pose those questions and prevent the same problem from happening twice.

You can take it a step further and change the way you think about problems. Most people don't want to deal with a situation that is overwhelming, irritating, and seems impossible to solve at first. However, if you decide to view those problems as a way to grow or as a challenge that will make you stronger, you will be less stressed about finding the needed solution. You will let your brain focus and break down the problem to analyze it in an easier way making you more flexible to deal with it and training you to solve future problems the same way. Your problems are opportunities to grow as a person they are lessons you need to be taught to protect from future hurt and pain.

You should also understand that not all problems are worth stressing over. For example, if your car doesn't start in the morning there is an obvious solution to that problem. Make a list of problems that have an actual negative impact on you and call them worst-case scenarios. Minor setbacks are not the end of the world and everything is happening to teach us something. If we take the example of your car not starting, next time you may think that you have to start a bit earlier for work than usual to catch a bus or the train if something like this happens again. This is a lesson you were taught because of a minor setback.

When you are facing a problem, simplify it by removing all the details. Go to the core of the problem. This way you will be able to find out the simplest and obvious solution to the problem that may have eluded you due to all the details you had to think of and maybe they weren't necessary to build your solution. It could also help to note as many solutions as possible for each problem, even the ones that you deem as ridiculous. With problem-solving, keeping an open mind is the very first element of finding the appropriate solution. Ridiculous solutions may lead you to the perfect one or even a ridiculous solution may be the one that needs to be adopted so as to solve the problem that is troubling you.

With each solution, you come up with, brainstorm the potential results both positive and negative. When you are finished doing this for each solution, choose the one that has a less negative impact according to your standards. If the choice you made was the wrong one, there is no need to beat yourself up about it. Embrace your mistakes and learn from them.

Problem-solving is not about getting always positive results. It's about solving your problems and even when choose the wrong solution, you are able to learn from it and apply your developed problem-solving skills more effectively next time. Also, if you another chance to fix the application of the wrong solution go back to choose a different one from the list you have made or make a new list of the positive and negative outcomes from each solution, using the new data you gathered from applying the first solution.

Apart from problem-solving skills, resilient people have a strong social circle that includes friends and family. Resilient people know the importance of support and have surrounded themselves with people that truly love them and would help them without aiming for any personal gain or having feelings of jealousy. Everyone that is close to resilient people truly cares about them and wish to see them succeed because a person who is resilient knows exactly what he or she needs and what they can offer to others.

They see themselves as survivors and not as a victim of a situation. Victimizing yourself will only make you depressed and lack any motivation for solving the problem at hand. Resilient people know that and by viewing themselves as survivors they are focusing on solving the challenges with determination, even when the situation seems impossible to solve. They are focused on attaining the most positive outcome given the circumstances, and there are many times they succeed in solving a problem effectively.

Another characteristic of resilient people is seeking assistance not only from people but from other sources too. For example, they read books about people who have gone through the same problems as them and how they managed to deal with it. They enrich themselves with the necessary knowledge to deal with any predictable or unpredictable challenged. When things get too rough for them, they join support groups to find people that are facing the same challenges as them and know how to provide the necessary support and compassion.

Enhance your resilience by finding a purpose in your life. There is no greater motivation to tackle any problems or challenges than to attain your life's purpose. Your mindset will immediately change and view those problems as lessons you need to be taught, especially if your goal and purpose are desirable enough for you. Trusting in your abilities and viewing them in a positive way is also a great way to develop your resilience. Have confidence in your ability to cope with stressful situations and to do that you need to start working on enhancing your self-esteem. Your strengths and accomplishments will be your tools and guide with which you will succeed in life.

To be resilient, you should be flexible and able to adapt to change. Embrace change and see them as an opportunity to learn new things and move your life to a new path. If everything stayed the same, people would be bored and not able to challenge themselves to becoming the best version of themselves. Understand that there will be setbacks on the road and view them with as much optimism as you can muster given the circumstances. There will be difficult times, but when those times are over, a brighter future will come and you will have the tools necessary to cope or even avoid a similar situation.

When you are faced with a difficult situation, it is easy to forget to take care of yourself. You may end up losing your appetite or eat too much, neglect exercising, not get enough sleep, and all these will come as a reaction to dealing with stress. Try to indulge in activities that make you feel good and loved. Even the simplest things can better your mood and let us not forget that self-care is an extremely important process to follow when you are building your emotional resilience. If you are not feeling good about yourself, you will not be able to control your emotions as effectively as you would under different circumstances.

Self-care may include you taking a relaxing bath filled with essential oils and scented soaps or nourishing your skin. You will have to follow a healthy diet and exercise regularly for your body to be prepared to face the stress levels associated with a difficult situation. If your body suffers, your mind will suffer too and by extent, your emotional resilience will not work.

When we wait for a problematic situation to pass without taking any action, we are only succeeding in prolonging the crisis. If you will not take immediate action to solve a challenge, you will end up being more stressed and never manage to find an effective solution to a problem that otherwise may have a simple way out. Whether or not the problem you are facing has a simple solution, you should focus on the progress you have made so far and plan your next move. This will keep you from being discouraged by everything that needs to be done until the problem is over. Keep working on the skills you have developed to achieve the emotional resilience needed for you to face your problems. When you find yourself lacking motivation, think of how your life will be much better the moment you will resolve the situation effectively.

Most resilient people face their fears straight on since this is the only way to deal with them effectively. When you avoid the things that scare you, they will make you more scared and the time will come when you will be forced to deal with them. It would be better for you to face them at the time you choose and you will be ready than to be forced to face them when you are not prepared and may make rash decisions. When you are forced and rushed into making a decision, chances are you will end up making a mistake. This is why emotionally resilient people face their fears from the start to avoid situations that will force them to make a mistake with severe implications for their future.

Appreciate what you have in your life and show gratitude towards other people and to yourself. You will be more resilient than ever before if you focus on the things you have accomplished rather than complain about the different choices you could have made or the things that you lost because you didn't follow a certain path or grabbed an opportunity at the appropriate time. Every choice we make opens a new path on which we should adapt and make the best of it. You can always change the things you don't like and resilient people know this. Instead of feeling depressed and complain about the things you weren't able to do, stop, make a plan, and make those dreams happen.

Making a list of your accomplishments and everything that you should be grateful for will help you develop this mindset and as time passes, this practice will be done automatically by you. For example you can make a weekly plan including a series of things to be grateful for such as things that you have that other people are not so fortunate to have, three goals you have set and accomplished during this week, three people that made you happy this week, six good things that happened to you this week, six things that you should be grateful to your family for, and what goals you would like to set for the plan of the next week.

By replacing negative thoughts with positive ones and maintaining a healthy lifestyle, you will see many things change during the course of your life. Be open to accepting criticism since this is the way for you to pinpoint your weak points and work on them. If you feel that there is nothing important in your life to challenge you and practice being resilient on, take up a new hobby or learn a new skill. It is extremely important for people to spend time with their family and friends. Resilient people have emotions too and a hard situation can affect them a lot, even though they refuse to give up. By spending time with the people you love and love you in return, you will be able to forget for a while the problems you are facing and focus on spending enjoyable moments that seem as a delightful break from the everyday stress.

It is a widely known fact that stress will affect your body and your ability to listen to it will suffer a considerable blow if you are not able to handle it. Emotional resilience will protect you and the progress you have made while trying to listen to your body, from having to start all over again. Apart from this emotional resilience, will help you be more aware of your potential and your emotions, therefore you will know how these emotions turn into a physical reaction. Searching for the different ways to deal with the problem at hand will only make you stronger, so don't forget to practice your problem-solving skills too.

Self-regulation is the final important skill we are going to analyze when it comes to handling your emotions, your stress levels, and therefore being free to listen to your body. As adults we are able to pretty much do everything we want at any time we want as long as we are within logical boundaries and we don't harm others. For example, we don't need to go to work every day, the vast majority of people will go to jail for skipping a day or two from work. Or we can eat cake or pizza for breakfast if that is what we desire. So, why are we going to work every day and why we prefer to eat pizza or cake for breakfast? How do we force ourselves to endure working on a day that this is the last place we would like to be in? How do we keep ourselves from not indulging in an unhealthy breakfast and we go for the healthy choice?

To the above questions, the answer is self-regulation, a process that most people follow without even thinking this is what they are practicing at a precise moment. Self-regulation is a skill that has to do with controlling our emotions, behaviors, and thoughts in favor of achieving the goals we have set for the future. This is why we are able to control our impulses of not going to work or eating an unhealthy breakfast. In other words, we are taught to think before we act, we practice self-control. A person who has developed self-regulation skills can keep his or her emotions under control and resist indulging in impulsive behaviors that might end up harming them. They can also cheer themselves up whenever they are feeling down and they can also match their emotional as well as their behavioral responses to the demands of their environment.

The ability to self-regulate in adulthood comes from our childhood since it is an important skill, children need to be taught for their emotional maturity and their future social interactions as they grow to be adults. Emotional self-regulation is the ability of a person to control or influence his or her emotions by taking the necessary steps to get himself or herself out of a bad mood or destress. Behavioral self-regulation is the ability of a person to act on behalf of his or her long-term goal and interests in a wat that is connected with his or her values. For example, you may not want to go to work, but you decide to go because you need money to live and know that it will reflect badly on your future goals if you aim for a promotion or to put some money aside to make your dreams happen.

Self-regulation will help both a child and an adult to control his or her cognitive impulses to respond to an uncomfortable feeling or environmental threats. For example, as a child, you may have been prone to throwing tantrums and grown into an adult who has learned how to tolerate the emotions that made you uncomfortable without having to resort to the behavior you had adopted as a child. Now, you are able to control your urges to act on emotions that make you uncomfortable and trigger a response that you have deemed as bad.

Self-regulation is a process in which we must be cautious of our behavior, the things that influence it as well as the consequences our behavior has on ourselves and our surroundings. Values are extremely important because we must judge our behavior according to our own standards as well as the standards presented by our broader environment. Also, we must ponder sometimes about what we think of our own behavior and the different ways we deal when faced with an important situation or decision. Do we often give in to our impulses? Do we let our emotions control our behavior which often leads us to make many mistakes?

In other words, you should take a pause and take some time between what you feel and your actions. Taking the necessary time between those two will let you think everything you are dealing with through, form a plan, and wait until your plan can be executed and wait for the results to become apparent. Children, as well as adults, may not find those steps easy to follow, but the problems caused by lacking the self-regulation skills will make anyone who wants to better his or her life develop them.

For example, a child who does not practice self-regulation will give in to his or her anger and may even resort to hitting other children out of frustration and that, in turn, will make him less able to maintain friendships and will face reprimands from his or her school. Most children resort to bullying due to this fact. They are not able to control their emotions that correspond to actions along with other psychological problems they may face. As far as children are concerned, they must be taught self-regulation skills or they are going to face many difficulties in their adult lives with behaviors that are developed from childhood.

Many adults suffer from poor self-regulation skills and self-confidence because they weren't taught as children how to develop those necessary abilities. Adults who lack those skills will have trouble handling stress and their anger. They are more prone to developing a mental disorder and they will develop anxiety disorders due to the fact that they will not be able to control their anger and other emotions such as sadness and fear. They may not even have a developed value system that would allow them to act according to it and they will have trouble expressing themselves appropriately. For example, if an adult values achieving in academics, he or she will not let themselves slack off before a test, in contrast to someone who will do so if he hasn't learned self-regulation.

Therefore, people face problems with self-regulation because their childhood was not ideal. He or she may have felt insecure and not as safe as they should. In other cases, where self-regulation problems were not caused by problematic childhood, the adult may not have followed the necessary strategies for managing feelings that would have made him or her uncomfortable. Self-regulation and self-control have a lot in common since they are very similar concepts. However, according to psychologist Stuart Shanker, they differ on two basic matters:

"Self-control is about inhibiting strong impulses; self-regulation is about reducing the frequency and intensity of strong impulses by managing stress-load and recovery. In fact, self-regulation is what makes self-control possible, or, in many cases, unnecessary."

Self-regulation is a more automatic process that happens in our subconscious unless a person chooses to monitor his or her behavior and feeling to control the self-regulation process. To further understand the concept of self-regulation, it is better to see what happens in action. Let us take a cashier who successfully remains calm and polite when he or she is berated from an angry customer for a situation he or she has no control over. Another example can be that of a child who does not throw a tantrum when he or she is told by the parents that he or she cannot have the desirable toy. A couple who is arguing about something important and decide to take some time to cool off can be another example of practicing self-regulation.

When it comes to listening to your body, an appropriate example is when you are trying to lose weight in order for you to be the best, healthier part of yourself, and you go out with a friend at a restaurant. While your friend may eat everything he or she wants, you decide to stick with the healthier choice because you know that eating unhealthy food will push back and affect your goals.

What can you do though to develop your self-regulation abilities? The first thing you can do and we have already analyzed is practicing mindfulness. With mindfulness, you will be able to place some distance between your emotions and reactions and focus on relaxation and calmness. Another strategy you can follow and will allow you to enhance your self-regulation abilities is cognitive reappraisal or else cognitive reframing. Cognitive reappraisal includes changing your mindset, in other words, the way you think about things. To be more specific, during this method you will have to interpret again a difficult and stressful situation you had to endure in order to alter your emotional response to it.

An example of such a case can be the fact that your good friend had not contacted you in days or even does not return your texts and calls. That will make you feel neglected and you will probably stress about him or her avoiding you or that he or she does not want to speak with you ever again. With cognitive reappraisal, you will think that your friend may be busy or is facing a problem with his or her own, instead of thinking that your friend hates you. If you practice cognitive reappraisal in your everyday life, you will be able to replace any negative emotions with positive ones and change your mind set for the better.

Some other effective strategies for self-regulation are acceptance of a situation and problem-solving skills, instead of avoidance, distraction, worrying, and suppression of emotions. The first step to self-regulation is to accept and recognize that people have a choice on how to react to every situation they face. More specifically, you have three options that include avoidance, attack, and approach. It is a fact that your feelings will lead to one path, but the truth is that you are not forced to listen to your feelings every time. You have control over them and behaving in a certain manner is your choice.

Then, you should monitor your body since this is the one, which will give you the necessary clues about how you are feeling, especially in cases, that your feelings are not apparent to you. For example, when your heart beats rapidly this may be a sign that you are entering a rage state or you are going through a panic attack. You should ask yourself if you are running away from difficult situations constantly. What are your emotions and your body's response during that time? Do you feel the need to scream in anger at someone who has hurt you or done something wrong? Will you get anything out of screaming your anger out or should you discuss the situation when you are calm? Start with building your boundaries and your value system rather than trying to suppress emotions. Try to see the larger picture and act in a way that will benefit you and the people around you.

Self-regulation is an integral part of emotional intelligence. According to Mayer's and Salovey's model of emotional intelligence, this ability is defined as:

"The ability to perceive emotions, to access and generate emotions so as to assist thought, to understand emotions and emotional knowledge, and to reflectively regulate emotions so as to promote emotional and intellectual growth"

According to expert Daniel Goleman, emotional intelligence is consisted of three parts, which are self-awareness, empathy, self-regulation, social skills, and internal motivation. Self-regulation, the ability to control or influence our emotions, is an essential part of emotional intelligence because the better we can understand and face our emotions and those of others, the better we will become to understanding the environment we find ourselves in and adapt to this environment which will result in pursuing our goals in a much easier way than before.

Usually, adults have problems practicing self-regulation at work because they are not able to handle their emotions under pressure. To better manage your emotions at work, you should do some breathing exercises; stay hydrated by drinking lots of water, eating healthy, and sleep at least eight hours a night. When you are trying to practice self-regulation, you should keep in mind some pointers that will help you succeed.

You should try to live your life with integrity by being a good role model for your family, friends, and to everyone, you associate yourself with. Live by the values you have adopted and try not to bend them for anyone. Be open to change and challenge yourself to deal with it in the best way that you can. If you find yourself struggling, work to improve your adaptation abilities and stay positive that you will succeed.

Identify what triggers certain behaviors by being aware of your strengths and weaknesses as well as what your limits are. When you pinpoint the triggers responsible for your bad behavior, try to change those behaviors by practicing meditation to stay focused and calm. Self-discipline is important when you want to achieve self-regulation. Work persistently towards your goals and that includes not reacting badly to every difficult situation you may face. If you react according to your emotions every time, you will face extreme setbacks that will make you lose any motivation to become what you always wished to be.

Take a step back from your thoughts and try to tackle the negative emotions associated with them, but never ignore your thoughts. Acknowledge them, analyze them, and try to solve the problems that are causing them. Letting go of negativity will open many opportunities for you and your mind will be clear to tackle effectively any task you will be given.

You will be able to think more clearly if you detach yourself from difficult situations and keep calm when you are asked to solve a problem. You will be able to consider the consequences of your actions. For example, what would happen if you did not follow self-regulation on a pressing matter and gave in to anger and frustration? Would the results of each course of action be different or would they remain the same? Keep in mind that there are also long-term consequences to your choices that will affect your future. If you keep thinking of this, you will be able to place some distance between your emotions and your actions.

Believing in yourself is the base of all self-regulation practices. You will need to work on your self-confidence and focus on your successes in life instead of pondering on your mistakes. Embrace failure, even though it is hard for many people to do so. Fear of failure is the most important reason why many people do not try to do the things they want because they are afraid of making a fool of themselves. However, if you think that challenging ourselves will help strengthen us and learn from both our success stories and failures, you will be ready to embark on any journey you wish to without having to worry about the ending.

By embracing your mistakes, you will take out the fear factor and be free to make your choices in accordance with your problem-solving skills. Challenging yourself little by little on a regular basis will help you built your confidence and personality. You could start by learning a new skill or taking up the hobby, you wished to do for so long. Do everything in your power to succeed in both the skill and hobby you love. Push your limits a little more every time and enhance your curiosity about what will happen when you succeed. If you do not succeed, you will gain the necessary knowledge and insight to try again and this time avoid the mistakes you did previously.

Listening to our bodies will be an easy thing to do by following everything we have analyzed so far. Before you start practicing the methods that will enable you to succeed in this goal you have set, you should always keep in mind that positivity is the right perspective of which we should view life. Negativity never helped anyone and caused harm to the people who decided to give in to it. According to Kendra Cherry, author of Very Well Mind, the definition of positivity is,

"Positive thinking actually means approaching life's challenges with a positive outlook. It does not necessarily mean avoiding or ignoring the bad things; instead, it involves making the most of the

potentially bad situations, trying to see the best in other people, and viewing yourself and your abilities in a positive light."

So, acknowledge that bit everything in life will go as you have planned them and be willing to make any effort necessary to realize your dreams even if you do not think they will pay off. Appreciate the good things life has to offer and grasp the opportunity you are given to develop a connection with your body. Do not forget that a positive attitude is considered the key to success because if you give in to pessimism and negativity you are surrendering your control to your emotions and will wallow in misery since you will be missing out an important opportunity you are given in leading a happy life through growth and development.

You want your body to respond to the connection you are trying to build with it in a positive way that will help you remain healthy for many years to come. If you approach this connection while maintaining negative emotions, it may as well shut you out, take the cue from you, and be less resilient and strong. Optimism when forging a connection with your body will reduce the chances of you developing depression and high levels of stress as well as bring you the happiness so many people crave to attain.

Epilogue

Listening to your body is not as easy or as hard as everyone would like to think. The truth is that no one ever told us as we were growing up how to listen and communicate with the only thing that we should take care of to be healthy, happy, and free to act however, you would like. We were taught only to listen to other people who knew better what our bodies want and we started reading stuff that was harming us by not only making us start counting calories, it made us also eat in ways that not enough energy was provided and as a result, someone may have felt tired all day long.

We need to stop trying to be thin and start listening to our bodies. The means to get thin, if they come from the wrong source, will make your body struggle to get all the nutrients it needs. The human body needs certain quantities of nutrients to function properly and only each body knows what is healthy for it and what is not. Embrace your body for all its faults and beauty and most of all respect it. Replace any possible negative thoughts you have of it with thoughts about being grateful to it for the way it works, for the way it keeps you protected and helps you function throughout the day.

Practice meditation and exercises we have analyzed throughout the course of this book to help you connect to your body and mind. If you find yourself, be skeptical about those practices, place a hand over your heart and feel it beat rhythmically. As you focus on that sound, close your eyes and try to feel the response of your body at the attention you are giving it. This will make you realize how important it is to start caring for the one thing that encompasses the reason you are alive.

Try to figure out what your body needs to stay healthy from now on. Maybe you need to exercise it, maybe you even need a new mattress to help you get a better night's sleep and relax it as much as you can. Taking small steps will help you stay committed to your goal. Find one thing at a time that your body needs and try to fix that before moving on to the next. For example, eat only when you feel hungry and not because it is time to eat. You might be comfortable eating six meals instead of three, and there is nothing wrong with that. Go with the flow, your body needs you to.

In addition, no one is telling you that it is wrong to snack, but instead of eating chips every day, you could buy vegetables, fruit or crackers and have a healthy snack. You can eat everything with moderation. Your body is not able to process a whole cake no matter how good it tastes and makes you feel. Try eating small portions of each food that you crave in order for your body to be able to process it. Do not let your feelings dictate the way you eat and take care of your body. Think of the food as the fuel you are giving to your car, you want your car to be given the best quality of fuel because it may develop serious functional problems in the future if given the lowest quality possible.

We are listening to our bodies when we are thirsty or want to go to the bathroom or when it needs sleep. It is not that hard to do that with other functions of our body. Keep in mind the skills needed to learn on how to listen to your body will take time to develop and practice as it happens with every other skill we decide to develop. If you find it hard keeping up with the cues your body is sending you, you could even start a journal and write about them.

Living in a noisy and stressful environment will make it harder to achieve this goal. Most people know they have to take care of their bodies, but they do not have the time. If you realize the importance and the benefits of being able to listen to your body and take care of it, you will realize that time is something you will be able to make for such an important task. So, be aware of the sensations and the cues your body is sending you to achieve a healthy lifestyle that will empower you to live with the best version of yourself.

Personal Notes

www.ingramcontent.com/pod-product-compliance
Lightning Source LLC
Chambersburg PA
CBHW051514030726
47592CB00006B/2257

9 781801 573580